Dedicated with gratitude and affection to
John Turner and Andrew Mayes, for their
friendship and support to John and to me,
both before John's death and since.

SO WRITTEN TO AFTER-TIMES

Compiled By Monica McCabe

'*By labour and intent study (which I take to be my portion in this life) joined with the strong propensity of nature, I might perhaps leave something so written to after-times, as they should not willingly let it die.*'

John Milton

Forsyth
Est 1857

SO WRITTEN TO AFTER-TIMES

Compiled by Monica McCabe

ISBN: 978-0-9514795-6-8

Published 2024 by the publishing division of Forsyth Brothers Limited
126 Deansgate, Manchester, M3 2GR, United Kingdom
forsyths.co.uk, 0161 834 3281.

Published with the support of The Ida Carroll Trust.

Front cover photo credit: Gareth Arnold.

Frontispiece photo: John at the age of about 12. Oil painting by Austin Davies, then husband of Beryl Bainbridge.

Back cover photo credits: Peter Thompson (John, green shirt); Doug Brady (John, monochrome); Melvyn Sillcock (Monica).

Book design by www.SiPat.co.uk. Typeset in Baskerville and Minion Pro.

Printed by LGP Print.

John McCabe CBE 1939–2015

John McCabe decided to be a composer at the age of five-and-a half. He studied in Manchester and Munich, while also from childhood studying piano with the great teacher, Gordon Green. He then embarked on an international career as composer and pianist. (His ground-breaking complete recording of Haydn's Piano Sonatas, now on 12 CDs, is regarded as a classic.) He has composed in almost every genre, including for film and television. Apart from full-length ballets like *Edward II* and the two full-evening ballets on the theme of King Arthur, his seven symphonies, many concertante works, symphonic poems and works such as *Notturni ed Alba* for soprano and orchestra place him at the centre of the repertoire. His output of chamber music, including seven string quartets, is equally outstanding and he made a significant contribution to the world of piano music. His many honours include the CBE, and he was twice awarded an 'Ivor' statuette, on the last occasion for Lifetime Achievement. He was also awarded the Iles Medal for his contribution to the brass band world, including his iconic work, *Cloudcatcher Fells*.

CONTENTS

FOREWORD

Letters can be both interesting and amusing. They can also be very revealing of character, more so than biography and even perhaps of autobiography. They may be carefully worked out and pored over, intended perhaps to be regarded almost as historical documentation, but they may equally be a carefree snapshot of the moment, whether in action or mood. They may illustrate the writer's interests, perhaps even prejudices, and the choice of language underscores his or her opinions and attitudes on many subjects. From letters gathered over a lifetime one can trace the development, for better or worse, of character. One can also note the incidents which have borne upon the writing of certain works. In John's case, for example, waiting, feeling somewhat stranded, for a lift in a Japanese city, outside an 'entertainment' venue with multiple mechanical jingles playing simultaneously produced, nearly 10 years later and near the end of his life, his brilliant little orchestral opener, Joybox (incidentally the first-ever Prom orchestral commission he was given). One can empathise, in various letters, with elation at having completed a work, and depression at 'writer's block'. Furthermore, letters will often express the character and ethos of the historical period.

I am fortunate in having inherited, from John and elsewhere, a large collection of letters, dating from his early childhood to his final, heart-breaking letter, written when desperately ill, and when the aggressive brain tumour was taking its toll on his ability to express himself, whether by speech or in writing. Many letters were written by John, to other musicians or to me; many others were written to John, often in answer. Some larger or smaller collections were handed back to me at different times, such as those to his friends of long-standing, George Odam and David Sternbach. David Matthews kindly returned copies of John's letters and shorter notes to him, when he heard that I was collating this book. Towards the end there are letters written by me on John's behalf, sometimes at his dictation. In some cases, later in the book, I have also drawn upon surviving emails, as this technology took over from written documents. The letters are presented in chronological order, as far as I have been able to judge. Richard Rodney Bennett and Alun Hoddinott, for example, seldom gave a full date for their letters. The selection here presents only a percentage of the trove of letters in my possession, which includes letters from such mighty names as Benjamin Britten, John Barbirolli, Georg Solti, Janet Baker, Charles Groves and John Lill. There are also many letters from composers such as John Joubert, Alun

Hoddinott or other musical personalities and performers. I have not chosen to select many letters simply because they were merely business-like, or were too private, or were in fact not particularly historically interesting. Addresses have been given where available, and where they no longer impinge upon more recent personal data. Not all letters, post-cards or emails provide addresses anyway, and some communications were written in transit. To avoid needless repetition addresses are given in full only on the first occasion they occur.

I have elsewhere expressed my gratitude and acknowledgement for the help I have received in gaining permission to publish these letters, whether directly from the writers or from their heirs, estates, foundations or trusts. I hope I have omitted no thanks where due, and apologise if I have done so. I would particularly like to thank Michael Finnissy for so generously allowing me to print letters from Richard Rodney Bennett to John and me which relate to his own music. I would also like to thank Jasper Conran not only for allowing me to print his letter, but also for graciously giving me permission to reproduce his beautiful costume designs for Isabella in the David Bintley ballet of Edward II.

A few words are due about my choice of letters, or parts thereof, and style of presentation. I have largely not included any standard greeting or farewell, as repetitively tedious and space-wasting. The material has been presented in most cases as a direct transcription of the writers' texts, including any idiosyncrasies. I have tended not to correct any misspellings or other errors, preferring to indicate them thus [sic]. Square brackets and dots […] represent the excisions that I have made from letters, for reasons of conciseness, privacy or lack of general interest in the content. Rows of dots without square brackets represent the writers' own. I made a decision not to use in headings any titles, honours, doctorates, professorships and so forth, on the grounds that they might not have been applicable at the time of writing, and it would be invidious to use them in one place and not in another; so I decided to banish them, however worthy the recipient, on the grounds that the intrinsic worth of the writer needs no embellishment.

Monica McCabe

January 2023

ACKNOWLEDGEMENTS

I would like to extend my gratitude to all those who are fortunately still with us at the time of writing this book for copyright permission to print their letters; and in the case of the great fashion designer, Jasper Conran, for graciously allowing me to reproduce his costume designs for Isabella in the David Bintley ballet, Edward II. For others, who are sadly no longer with us, I would like to thank the following heirs, estates or trusts:

Alan Rawsthorne (Rawsthorne Trust); William Alwyn (William Alwyn Foundation); Harold Truscott (Guy Rickards); Peter Racine Fricker (Un. of S. California, D. Seubert, also C.J. Husted); Nicholas Maw (Maija Hay); Richard Rodney Bennett (Meg Peacocke); Robert and Angela Simpson (Helen Reynolds); Barney Childs (Un. of Redlands, California, J. Modica, Sanjeet Mann); Steve Martland (Phil and Elsie Toland); Alan Bush (Maeve O'Higgins); William and Yvonne Mathias (Rhiannon Mathias); Patrick Thomas (Helen Thomas); Maj. Peter Parkes (Jonathan Parkes); Ursula Vaughan Williams (VW Charitable Trust); Beryl Bainbridge (Estate of Beryl Bainbridge); Alun Hoddinott (Rhiannon Hoddinott); Derek Bourgeois (Norma Bourgeois); Stephen Oliver (Jim Oliver and other family members); Thomas Pitfield (Pitfield Trust); Gerard Schurmann (Carolyn Schurmann); Sidonie Goossens (Jennie Goossens); Julian Bream (Julian Bream Trust, Antony Bream, Jan Burnett); John Joubert (Mary Joubert, Anna Joubert); Joseph Horovitz (Anna Horovitz); Jane Manning and Anthony Payne (Dominic Saunders, Richard Montgomery); Barbara Rawsthorne (Rawsthorne Trust); James Loughran (with the kind help of Dawn Durrant and David Salgo); Benjamin Britten (BrittenPears Arts); Sir Charles Groves (Sally Groves); Anthony Hodges (Mrs P. Hodges); Richard Evans (with the kind help of Andrew Blackledge).

I hope I have not forgotten to thank anyone, or make acknowledgements where they are due. If I have, I apologise and say that every effort has been made to gain permission where it has been possible. In some cases I have found it impossible to contact heirs or estates. If further information is received at a later date an appropriate acknowledgement will be included. The extensive material from David Sternbach and George Odam was kindly provided by them with publication in mind. However, I must further thank Penelope Odam and Timothy Odam for their permission.

1948–1965

From Frederick H. Wood (organist)
February 2nd 1948
(Typed)

252, Hornby Road,
Blackpool.

Thank you for your letter. When I saw the three soldiers marching on one sheet, and a fairy sitting on a toadstool on the other, I wondered if you had been writing a Soldiers' March and a Fairy Dance, for the piano. I am sure they would both be easier to write than a symphony, and besides you could play them whenever you wanted, instead of having to wait for a band to come along and play your symphonies […] Yes, when you are well and strong, I hope you will come to Blackpool as you say, and let me play the organ for you […] I am sending you a photograph of the organ as it looks inside the Church. They are all 'speaking pipes' – I mean that none of them are 'dummies' put there for show. The longest you can see is 16 feet long…..You can keep all the photos. Organ music, by the way, is written on three staves – two for the hands, like piano music, and below them another stave for notes played by the feet, on what we call the Pedals. I have heaps to show you when you come […]

Lines from a long and very kindly letter, replying to the still only 8-year-old John.

John with parents and maternal grandparents (German-born). Photo probably in Huyton, near Liverpool, c. 1941.

John, aspiring child composer. He later threw away his childish writings, saying he didn't know what he was doing at that time, but was fascinated by music.

To his Mother
28/8/58
(Hand-written)

8, Sebmore Avenue,
Hayling Island

[…] As I write the thunder and lightning are rolling and whistling round the house, and the rain and wind are lashing the trees. Yesterday it was wonderful, & I enjoyed the journey […] Michael [*his cousin*] is upstairs practising his trumpet, which he got for £3 a few weeks ago. He's remarkably good. He bought Haydn's Trumpet Concerto a week ago & can play the slow movement quite well. The 1st movement is a bit sticky, but not bad, but the 3rd is too difficult. I said I tried to write something for him, & I have tried but failed.

They have an enormous number of records here. Lots of Klemperer Beethoven, Schumann's 4th Symphony, Mendelssohn's Italian, etc. This morning I played some of my music to them (except Uncle Boy of course): The Rivals music, Bagatelles, and Music for Piano. The last puzzled them a bit, but the others went down very well […]

John was, and remained, very close to this family of cousins, living on Hayling Island on the south coast of England. Uncle Boy (otherwise Uncle Ernest) was the youngest in the family of John's father. While musical, clearly he was not a fan of contemporary music. Michael was I think teaching himself to play the trumpet.

From Humphrey Procter-Gregg
29.9.60
(Hand-written)

37, West Heath Drive, N.W. 11.

Very glad to get your letter & hear that you really enjoyed your visit – we were certainly pretty active, but I'd half-begun to wonder whether the discrepancies in a number of our personal tastes had not "put you off" a bit!

There are, I hope fortunately, a number of points on which we can feel at sympathy & I wish there were more! I feel I could be more use to your development (let alone enjoying each other's company more) if you had a rather broader outlook on the world outside the contemporary camp – and there is an awful lot of the world - all the past, much of the present & I hope a lot of the future, quite outside the contemporary craze of democracy for the anti-traditional: that craze is what seems to <u>me</u> a narrow outlook - & you probably think my own outlook narrow! - which is a large part of our difficulty. When I was your age I tried to be enthusiastic, or at any rate keenly interested in modern art & culture, but after trying for thirty years, I've grown more & more to feel that, against the background of great historical periods of culture & their remains in our libraries, galleries & museums, the present phase is crude and barbarous & not really artistic or cultured at all, merely the expression of self-assertiveness by people with pretty insensitive eyes, ears and perceptions! […]

Humphrey Procter-Gregg was John's composition teacher at Manchester University. John was studying piano as well as composition, and already playing music by such as Nielsen, Copland, Webern and even Carter. The relationship with his teacher broke up after John performed a piece of his own music in a recital at his old school, the Liverpool Institute in Liverpool, without Procter-Gregg's 'permission'. John once said to me that the trouble was that HPG (as he was usually known) felt that Music had finished with Puccini's Turandot. This may have been an exaggeration. The inter-generational struggle depicted in this letter is rather sad, and in its plaintive expression, touching.

4

To George Odam
April 16 1961
(Hand-written)

139, Manchester Rd.,
Altrincham,
Chesh.

[…] I must now dash (as in -) but before I do, 2 musical items:

1) The BBC Northern Orchestra played "Sinfonia da Requiem" brilliantly in Liverpool (George Hurst), but only lukewarm applause, for what I think is a masterpiece.

2) The BBC Symphony concert from Venice (did you hear it?) convinced me of the beauties of the "Nocturne". I was amazed to hear VW's 4th most heartily booed (a fine work, too) but the performances on the whole were pretty poor.

Have finished my Violin Concerto, at long last!

John sketched his Violin Concerto (No. 1) in the Lake District, just before starting at Manchester University. He finished the orchestration while a student. George Odam was a fellow-student, and remained a life-long friend.

John on the Wirral, NW England, aged about 20, at the time he wrote his Violin Concerto No. 1. Photo: Doug Brady c. 1959. **4**

To his Mother
August 10 1961
(Hand-written)

21, Greenfield Close,
Stapleford,
Cambridge.

[…] My interview went off very well. I was interviewed by E.E.E. himself, and he told me that he was "quite impressed". I would have to start out as a trainee for a while on a wage of £700 and gradually take on my full responsibilities. The job sounds right up my street. The only thing is that he would want me to start in about 3-4 weeks!

He is an old acquaintance of Mr Cox & the suggestion is that I should talk to Mr Cox as soon as possible about it, and see whether I could forego my last College year. It seems a pity, but this job is a fine opportunity. It's all very difficult. Anyway, after seeing Mr. Cox, I shall write to E. E. E. & tell him what gives. He can then decide if he will take me on, if I'm available.

The Prom was extremely good, the Stravinsky superb. We spent the day wandering around London, & after the Prom dashed across London & caught our train (the last one) with 2 minutes to spare (and then it was late leaving). On Monday, we spent hours cycling around this lovely countryside & played cricket in the evening. Since then I've been very stiff.

John usually addressed his mother as 'Dear Ma' and she signed herself as Ma. I can shed little light on this letter and the interview. I don't know what the job was, or who E.E.E. was. I believe that this was around the time that John's father, Frank, got considerably into debt. He was by now I think running two households, as there had been a partial separation between Frank and Elisabeth, who followed John to Manchester when he became a student there. Also I believe that Frank was made redundant from his scientific job around this time, so John probably felt a need to be self-supporting. However, the Cambridge job was never taken up. Mr Cox was Principal of the Royal Manchester College of Music, as it then was. He thought highly of John's abilities and possibly persuaded him to continue his education.

6

To his Mother
30 Sept. 1964
(Typed)

Hochschule für Musik,
8 München 2
Arcisstrasse 12,
Germany.

It was nice to arrive at the Hochschule this morning and find some letters await-ing me; thank you! This morning I began the long process known as registering at the Hochschule. God, what a business. The offices […] used to be Hitler's offices in München, and the officials behave as if he were still in power. I had to ring [Harald] Genzmer up (he was just on the point of leaving town) to get him to agree that I could take my first month's allowance out. Then I had to run back to the office to get them to ring him up before he left town in order that he could tell them that I was genuine! […] I am not taking first-study piano. This has now become clear; I am not entirely sorry, as the young American who lives […] in the same house as I doesn't appear to think much of most of the teachers. It seems that they do what I've always kept clear of: concentrate on the basic classics […] The composition course includes 4 hours of counterpoint and fugue each week, and numerous other dainties like that […]

Many thanks for your resume of Rawsthorne's talk; he seems to have been in his usual pleasantly sardonic form! […]

Can you send me the violin part to the violin concerto? It's amongst my music somewhere, and it's not heavy; don't register it or anything, just pop it in an envelope. I need it for completing the dynamics in the piano score and making a new copy perhaps for Novellos […]

In view of John's unflattering remarks about Munich it is worth remembering that his mother was in fact German. She and her family suffered during the First World War. Her father, living and working in England, was interned for the dura-tion, and the family were separated. John had hoped very much to study for a post-graduate year with Karl Amadeus Hartmann, but sadly he was dying. John did not like his substitute, Harald Genzmer, and neither was he impressed with his piano teacher.

To David Sternbach
October 15th 1964
(Typed)

München-Gräfelfeing,
Akilindastrasse 11,
Germany.

[…] As you will see, I have an address, without a piano, but on Nov. 6th I'm moving downstairs to share with an American pianist […] whose family is leaving for the States on that day; he has a piano, which I can use when he's not there, which is probably not very often, but it's cheap and I will have the occasional use of a piano. More than that I don't think I could expect. I live, as appears to be my unintentional habit, out of the city, 20 minutes by train, but there is a good service, & it is cheap if you get a monthly ticket.

So I appear to be settled straight off; the Auslandsstelle gave me this address as soon as I arrived in Munich, thinking that it would be only until the end of Oct., but I've wangled that I can stay here permanently. It is right out in the country, and I can do lots of work here, despite the spiders (I spent a few days in the cellar, which was alive with the bastards […]) Every night I fight my way through a fog of webs; no, it is not quite as bad as that, and I'm really quite frohlich, or something. […]

Fidelio seems to be on everywhere, incl. here. I haven't been to the opera yet, due to pressure of work, and also lack of money (I'm still awaiting the extra 300 Marks that I'm supposed to receive when I arrive here! I've got my monthly allowance, but this extra payment to help me settle in has not come; and I had to pay 83 Marks just to enrol at the Hochschule, which is bloody ridiculous; I'm going to write my second, rather less polite letter to my scholarship board today, since I last wrote two weeks ago, and that has given them sufficient time to do something about my money!). Please excuse the Faulkner-type sentence construction).)…!

PS [*hand-written*] It's rather comical that my nickname in Manchester was "Cabe". Here, the officials call me Mr Cabe, despite frequent corrections, & my post at the Hochschule is put under C!

John's friendship with the American horn-player, David Sternbach, whom he met while studying in Germany, lasted all his life. Correspondence soon fell into a student-ish, ragging mode, and largely stayed there. David had a very quick-fire sense of humour. John remained living in this curious household throughout his year in Munich. He had to sleep in the cellar/boiler-room whenever the daughter of the house came home, as he seems to have occupied her bed-room. He once described the house (and household) as being like something out of Hansel and Gretel.

8

From Alan Rawsthorne
5 April 1965
(Hand-written)

Sudbury Cottage,
Little Sampford,
Saffron Walden,
Essex.

Thank you for your letter; please forgive me for not replying sooner. And thank you most sincerely for the dedication; I am truly touched and delighted by this, and look forward greatly to getting to know the Trio. Is there a performance in the offing? I was in Liverpool a few weeks ago, when they did my Symphony, and stayed a couple of nights with Gordon and Dorothy […] I'm interested to hear about the music in Munich. The Germans, at least, are still deep in the grand Romantic Tradition, don't you think? – and invented the 12-note system to make it nice and tidy. I often feel that Henze could break into the Ride of the Valkyries without much difficulty. Is Hartmann still producer at the Opera? Isabel worked with him when she did the designs for Elektra at Covent Garden. […]

John's String Trio was dedicated to Alan Rawsthorne on his 60th birthday. Rawsthorne was close friends with Gordon and Dorothy Green, which is how John first met him, as a child. Gordon Green was John's piano teacher. Isabel Rawsthorne, Alan's wife, was previously married to Constant Lambert, and before that was the muse, and possibly mistress, of several great artists.

9

To George Odam
Apr. 11/65
(Hand-written)

Altrincham

I'd be delighted to do a recital for you […] probably in the autumn term. […] I'm in Germany again from May 8 – July sometime […] and would like to have the summer in which to revive repertoire & perhaps learn some more stuff (practice is minimal in Deutschland). The sort of programme I'd most like to play would be rather odd (as you might expect): some modern works of varying styles, and some Haydn (& possibly Schubert if there's time). I've developed a great passion for Haydn, esp. the piano sonatas, of which I play several, and would very much like the opportunity of doing 2 or 3 of them in one programme. […] could you possibly let me know possible dates, or days of the week, that might be suitable? I have a number of first performances in the autumn term […] and am anxious to be there. In particular the Halle are doing a new piece in their mid-week series, possibly in Nov. (or Feb – March) […] Before I return to Germany, I have one or two recitals, including the delightful but frightening task of playing Rawsthorne's piano works at a Manchester concert in honour of his 60th birthday, with the composer present. It's a pity he hasn't written a solo work for piano recently, because in the last few years he seems to have written some of his best stuff (inc. the 3rd Symphony […]

PS Suggested modern composers from whom work could be chosen: Tippett, Richard Bennett, Rawsthorne, Copland, Webern, Schönberg (Op. 19 only), Ken Leighton, Hoddinott, Britten, and even one McCabe.

Surprisingly John says in this letter that George had converted him to Britten's music by playing him The Turn of the Screw, this despite his remark in an earlier letter about the Sinfonia da Requiem, and the fact that he regarded his visit as a child to see Peter Grimes as one of the great events of his life. The new McCabe piece was probably the Variations on a Theme by Hartmann, premiered in the Free Trade Hall, November 24 1965, with Maurice Handford conducting. George Odam was by this time teaching in a college in Bath, and able to offer John recital opportunities.

10

To David Sternbach
April 30/65
(Hand-written)

Altrincham

[…] What I'm doing is learning a huge pile of difficult music in too short a time, hence my inability to swing South and beat your head in. One recital over, successfully (except for a Liszt piece; why do I try stuff I can't play? Rest of programme was fine, best perf. I've given of the Copland Sonata, which went down extremely well with a rather conservative audience!) but next Tuesday is Doomsday. A mid-day recital in town (Mozart & Brahms, incl. the latter's Sonata in C, which is a fiend & requires 8 hands), evening concert in Manchester (Rawsthorne piano music, with the composer present, which is unnerving). All new stuff, & not much time […]

John's letter explains why he is unable to travel from Manchester to London to meet David, currently in the UK. His letter, as often to David at this time, is student-ish

John with Barbirolli and his mother Elisabeth, around the time of his First Symphony. Cheltenham Festival 1966. **10**

and hyperbolic. Unusually for him, it is also slightly ribald. The combination of two concerts in one day, one in London and the other in Manchester, is certainly un-nerving, but an aspiring young performer must take on what he is offered.

1966–1973

11

From Benjamin Britten
27th December 1967
(Typed, but signed by Britten)

The Red House,
Aldeburgh,
Suffolk.

I have just looked at my NOTTURNO in relation to the points you raise. I suggest that the two chords you find unplayable should be very quickly spread. This is, to my mind, much preferable to a deliberate spread with one note before the others, and certainly preferable to changing the notes. What I do suggest, however, is that you play all the chords at the beginning of these bars in a similar way; it will sound less strange than having one spread, and the others 'sec' […]

John's narrow spread of four fingers, and wide thumb spread, combined with long fingers, caused piano-playing problems. His recording of Britten's Notturno is still available on a Naxos CD.

12

From Alan Rawsthorne
25th February 1968
(Hand-written)

Saffron Walden

By now I sincerely trust that you will have received all of the quintet, and I do apologise for its having come off the assembly lines, as it were, unassembled. Here are a few notes about metronome marks, but please don't take them too literally.

There follow a series of suggested metronome marks, and a correction of a note in the cello part after P, with a few other remarks.

13

To George Odam
March 10 1968
(Typed)

106, Richmond Rd.,
Cardiff.

[…]Western Theatre Ballet did a ballet (Danse Macabre) to my Symphony this week, and it was absolutely splendid. Most melodramatic and gloomy, but very exciting […]

This is the first example of a ballet being made to John's music, in this case what became his First Symphony. He was always very amused by the title. Western Theatre Ballet was directed at the time by Peter Wright, later founder of the Birmingham Royal Ballet, and knighted. One of the dancers, Elaine MacDonald, later created the title role in the ballet Mary, Queen of Scots, Peter Darrell/John McCabe/Scottish Ballet 1975-76.

14

To Monica Smith
Dec. 17 1968
(Typed)

49, Burns Avenue,
Southall,
Middlesex.

Very many thanks for your letter, which I was delighted to receive. I'm very glad you wrote as you did, because it encourages one to think one's basic approach is right, and for somebody who is not a professional journalist but almost a spare-time writer, this is very important.

I think if I have, and am able to put across, a good understanding of music, this is entirely due to the fact that I am first and foremost a musician. I don't regard writing reviews lightly, of course, but it is nevertheless almost peripheral to my main activities, and if the time ever came that I had to make a choice between the two, I would have to give up reviewing, tho' I can't see any reason why this should happen for many years. After all, I think it impossible to be busier than I have been the last few months, yet I seem to have managed to get everything done. But writing from a vantage point within the musical profession does give one a considerable advantage; it's obviously hard to avoid grinding one's favourite axes, but I try to avoid this and on the whole I don't think I fall into this trap (but since I like most music anyway to some degree, it's easier for me than for someone who only likes Gesualdo and Stockhausen).

When I say that I've been very busy the last few months, I mean it. Since the beginning of September I've done the full score and vocal score of an opera, a complete harpsichord concerto, a short concertino for piano duet and orchestra, and an oboe quartet as well as playing about a dozen concerts. Naturally I'm feeling a bit tired of composing suddenly, but now my attention turns to concentrate on piano playing, with occasional compositional excursions, for a while, and I find this constant change of emphasis refreshing. I think I can do more work if I've got to change occasionally like this than if I were simply a composer or a pianist; and writing about music, I'm quite sure, gives another angle on things which is helpful and often illuminating, apart from being enjoyable in its own right, so I shall continue to review as long as they want me to, if I can. [...]

This letter pre-dates our relationship. I had written to John saying how much I enjoyed his reviews and articles in Records and Recording magazine, for which I was then working. I said that they always made me want to listen to the records in question. The opera John mentions was his children's opera, The Lion, The Witch and The Wardrobe. John's composing and performing activities during the next years were indeed prodigious, and he was shortly to make a major national breakthrough with his work for soprano and orchestra, Notturni ed Alba.

15

From John Barbirolli
1st January 1970
(Typed and signed)

Walton Lodge,
4, New Hall Road,
Salford M7 0EL,
Lancashire.

As you know, I was in Houston at the time of my birthday, and as soon as I returned became extremely busy with rehearsals and performances of Messiah and other things, and unfortunately over the Christmas holidays I had to take to my bed with a most beastly attack of bronchial asthma and am only just beginning to come round although I hope to be able to leave for Italy on Saturday for a series of concerts there.

I was touched by all you have to say about the Otello recording and deeply moved by the way you have expressed this. It is a work I have great admiration for and I think in some ways one of the greatest operas ever written in view of its perfect proportions, length, libretto etc.

Thank you so much for writing, and forgive this brief note, but I have so much to try to get done before I leave.

Barbirolli was a warm and generous supporter of John as a young composer. He was especially supportive over the matter of John's First Symphony, which a reading panel at the BBC did not pass for performing. Barbirolli suggested that if they refused to accept it he would not record for the BBC again. His letter begins with the very warm greeting, 'My dear John' and ends with 'Warmest good wishes from us both'.

16

To George Odam
13.6.70
(Typed)

Southall

Just a short note […] to say that I hope you still have your Japanese wind-chimes, because the CBSO can't get hold of any and I've suggested that they write to you and ask you if you can help; if you don't want to lend yours but know where they could get some, perhaps you could let them know […] They are also having difficulty getting wind wood chimes, but I think the Liverpool Phil should be able to help there, as they used them in a Ginastera work last season. I don't think I'm terribly popular with the CBSO for this, as they have also had to hire a set of chromatic crotales, and they wanted to cut down the budget for this concert! [...]

This has been a rather depressing week for me, because my Liverpool Phil work for harpsichord and orchestra, which was supposed to go on at the Festival Hall last night, didn't happen; the soloist strained a tendon in his right hand and the first performance of this work, for the 2nd time, has had to be postponed. Since I've heard a rehearsal of the orchestral part & am very satisfied with that [...] this is an inauspicious beginning to the work's career, but we must just hope that next time it goes ahead [...]

The Three Choirs Festival work, Notturni ed Alba, with soprano Sheila Armstrong and the City of Birmingham Symphony Orchestra conducted by Louis Frémaux, was an instant success. It received many performances, and was later recorded, with Jill Gomez as soloist. This recording is still available on CD. Metamorphosen, for harpsichord and orchestra, was cancelled a third time by the soloist, Rafael Puyana, and John took over as soloist at 24 hours' notice, receiving a quick lesson beforehand on playing the harpsichord, from Bridget Fry.

17

From Frederic Cox
17th August 1970
(Hand-written PS on typed letter)

Royal Manchester College of Music,
Devas Street,
Oxford Road,
Manchester M15 6FX.

[...] I only wish that you had made Manchester your home & you were still with us. Still we may have you back one day! I hope all goes well with you & that the future holds in store the success you [indecipherable word] merit. It was nice seeing your mother at the party.

Frederic Cox had been the Principal of the Royal Manchester College of Music during John's time there as a student. John had obviously not been able to attend his leaving party.

18

From Andre Previn
6th November 1970
(Typed and signed)

No address given

Thank you very much for seeing to it that the score of your Notturni ed Alba was sent to me so promptly. I admire the piece very much, and I hope it pleases you to hear that it is definitely scheduled for our '71 – '72 season. I will, of course, have to get some dates from Sheila, but we should be able to fix an absolute date very soon. I look forward to conducting the work very much.

Some time I would love to play through the Rachmaninov 2-piano suites with you. I will be playing them in the summer of '72 with Ashkenazy at the Queen Elizabeth Hall, but to tell you the truth I have so far never seen them.

My remembrance is shaky about whether or not this play-through did take place, but I think it did happen, at London's South Bank, some time in 1971. Subsequently an LP recording was made, and I have a copy of this. Sheila Armstrong had premiered Notturni ed Alba.

19

From Frederic Cox
22-11-70
(Hand-written)

86, The Downs,
Altrincham,
Cheshire

[…] I can't let time go by without telling you what <u>very great</u> pleasure your very generously worded letter gave me. It is a tribute that I shall value above all others – though I agree it would have been nice to see you, it is more heart-warming to have something tangible that one can read & re-read with so much pleasure!

You exaggerate of course: wherever you had received your musical education you would have got to the top. It is a source of real satisfaction that I might to a certain extent have been the cause - & an infinitely greater source of satisfaction that you have <u>set down in writing</u> your acceptance of the fact! I hope you go from success to success.

To George Odam
May 7 1971
(Typed)

Southall

[…] My own work is concerned currently with the 2nd symphony; I have a couple of performances in Farnham next week (one of a new piece which is a bit dull really) but in general I'm concentrating on the symphony. I've done two movements, each in a couple of days but with a lot of walking about and playing bits on the piano before getting down to writing; these are the scherzo and one of the slow movements (I think the 2nd as the first will have to be more sustained and static, as well as rather more peaceful, after a first movement that I hope will emerge as quite powerful). The scherzo is one of my usual jolly little tunes [*sic!*] with lots of syncopation and so on; the slow movement that I've done is rather vehement, at any rate at the climax and it rises up to this with the use of an extremely exotic convoluted cello tune complete with exotic appoggiaturas and things, rather a departure for me and I think it comes off, though I have to make some changes when I go back to the work when I've got it all sketched out and go through it in order to have second thoughts about bits of it. As far as I can see, it's definitely in 5 movements, played continuously; well, not always movements because this slow movement, for instance, though a large single division within the overall work is not really separable from the rest; it forms part I hope of an indivisible whole. Forgive me for going on so long about this piece, but I'm very involved with it just now, and although what I've done can with a few changes be made quite good, I'm very exercised in my mind about stylistic problems. This is because it's too easy to fall into the trap of repeating oneself (one's earlier pieces) too easy to take an easy way out when writing a quick movement that is a gradual crescendo (as the 1st and 5th are). Furthermore, these two, because so similar (deliberately) in technique must be given different identities in style without breaking the unity of the whole piece. I don't think I've ever faced quite this problem before, because I've never written an orchestral work of this size which has used the formal devices of my chamber music (where I've at last got to a state where the various divisions do make a single unit, a form I like because you get variety and unity at the same time). I've written the end of the symphony, anyway, and I know roughly how to get there, but it's filling in the gaps that is going to be tricky. I hope I'll get a chance to play through the piece to you when I've finished sketching, because I'd value your views on it (even if you don't like Notturni!)

Of course, a lot of the difficulties are emotional, because some of my self-confidence has gone. I'm constantly walking around trying to tell myself that even if the musical problems of this piece are slightly different to any that I've encountered before in an orchestral work, there's no reason why I shouldn't solve them as easily as usual, but I'm always doubting the validity of what I'm doing. Not on the grounds that I'm stylistically old-fashioned and therefore invalid, because I don't really think that's true (partly because I'm still developing anyway and therefore am not sitting down having found a particular style and writing the same piece all the time), but on the grounds that I don't altogether believe in myself any more. I depended on Hilary an enormous amount (this isn't a new discovery, I always knew it, and I thought she did, but she can't have done), and to have such a source of musical self-confidence taken away so suddenly and at such a time was a real blow (apart from any other considerations such as emotional ones, though they too play a part, obviously). But it has affected my ability to work properly, there's no doubt, and even though I've managed to get in some spells of hard work on this piece I'm constantly afraid of getting down to any more because I'm literally afraid of the results, which is something that's never happened to me before. Perhaps too it's the result of the pressure now that my career seems to be taking a sudden upsurge again (practically every one of my main orchestral works is getting at least one performance next season, and Notturni is having at least 5 by 3 different conductors), and I'm always aware that this symphony is probably going to be recorded, so it's got to be good. That knowledge doesn't help! I faced the problem in a lesser way once before, because when the Halle commissioned the 1st symphony it was because the Hartmann Variations had been so successful, so the symphony had to be good if not better (I think it's actually better, though it's rather different and thus difficult to compare); but that was at a lower level really (in the sense that a recording is international whereas this was basically a local thing which might not have gone beyond local confines had the symphony turned out to be a flop). Anyway, I suppose one just presses on and gets things done as usual. Of course, one of the problems is that although I like being alone part of the time (and obviously have to be to compose) I hate living alone; I desperately need someone there, and someone who is in sympathy with what I aim at in music. The obvious answer is to find someone, but of course that's easier said than done, and although I'm intermittently having what is known as "a good time", that's not the answer in the long run. But I'm damned if I'm going to go out into the market place and look for a slave, which has been suggested by one or two people. Perhaps I should put an advert in OZ or IT for a beautiful Swedish au pair girl who likes modern music…

Anyway, enough of this; I can't think how I got on to this, because I didn't intend to. It's curious that you should remark (as many other people have) that I was looking so well and relaxed, because I had a terrible time a few days afterwards; a kind of delayed reaction, I suppose, made worse by the constant pressure of work as well as emotion over the months. However, that is I hope behind me now; the one thing that's really going to make life difficult emotionally is my mother, because although I'm managing to keep her at arm's length most of the time it is simply impossible to tell her straight out that she must not interfere and I must live my own life, because all she will do is get in a rage, probably have a black-out (which will of course be directly caused by my ungratefulness and so on), and proceed to start where she left off again. I fully intend to move, though this is a process I'm hardly capable of tackling properly and I'm certainly not looking forward to it; I fully expect her to be disappointed at this because I suspect she might suggest coming down here one of these days. The campaign has vaguely started with hints about how life is very difficult for her financially; she's often talked about moving herself if her rent goes up, and I'm sure she wants me to offer one of these days for her to move here. She might well say no at first, because she wants to stress that she has her own life to lead in Manchester, and so on, but I hope it never gets to the state where she asks directly to come here. It does sound ungrateful, I know, but it would be absolutely impossible; and at the risk of being made to sound rather nasty, I simply couldn't put up with it. Despite all she's done for me, and despite her ill-health (and although she's usually all right, she does have her black-outs, and the fall she had at Newton Park did quite a lot of internal damage) her presence here would be fatal to me in every way. I'm not quite as selfish as that usually, but in this case I have to be in order to survive, I know that.

Enough of all this; God knows why I write at such length about these things. I must get on with some work. I hope we'll meet again soon, and that I'll hear your tape very soon. [...]

John opens his heart about all his emotional problems, in a way that is very rare. He is obviously in a fever of excitement about his very powerful Second Symphony, but much of his letter is about the trauma of the break-up of his short-lived marriage to the young composer, Hilary Tann. There are to me several surprises in his letter: firstly that he is playing material on the piano, at this early stage, something that he did not do later on. Secondly he is hopeful of and willing to play through the work to another person, and take advice. He was much more self-reliant when I knew him. Thirdly I am somewhat surprised at George Odam's not liking Notturni ed Alba, and wonder why. It was a popular success from the beginning. The emotional difficulties with his mother remained with him all her life.

To Monica Smith
23/11/71
(Hand-written)

No address

This seems to be the only piece of paper I can lay my hands on, there being hotel envelopes but no paper. I was delighted to get your message (yesterday) & your letter (today); the letter is certainly the nicest I've ever had! […]

Your letter was really encouraging, as well as lovely, & it has helped considerably to make me feel less worried about tonight. I'm still worried, of course, in fact very nervous indeed as always, but there's a certain element of looking forward to it also. This is certainly due in part to the fact that Rudi Schwarz does the piece well, & takes the finale at a speed with which I can cope, and also I think you'll be surprised at the actual sound of the music, because although it's a small orchestra it sounds quite colourful, & one thing about it surprises me, which is that I don't feel the lack of percussion; when I come to do the full orchestra version percussion will make it sound completely different. At present, though there is no percussion, it almost sounds as if there is! […]

I've just been moving heaven & earth trying to get a room for my mother tonight; there is a Hotel Booking Service in N/castle, but this town is absolutely booked out, & they've finally managed to get one at a motorway hotel just outside Gateshead! We'll be given a lift back after the concert; I'm being met at 2.0 & going in the same car as the great Kyung Wha Chung, no less. […]

John and I got together in September 1971, yet I knew virtually nothing of John's music at this time (knowing him largely as a writer on music and a pianist) so the sound might well have surprised me, with or without percussion. This occasion was the premiere of John's Piano Concerto No. 2 'Sinfonia Concertante', in Middlesborough Town Hall on 23rd November 1971, with John as soloist and the Northern Sinfonia conducted by Rudolf Schwarz. I was not there, as I was working in London, but I did attend the performance in Oxford, which I believe was the second. What really did surprise me, returning to his letter, is that John thought of making a full orchestral version of the concerto. He never did, probably being just too busy.

22

To George Odam
February 6th 1972
(Typed)

Southall

Many thanks for your letter at Christmas. It is high time I answered, and as I seem actually to have some time to spare for answering correspondence today, this is a good time! […] Your remark about not finding the avant-garde as frightening after the previous year contrasts with my own feelings; I find them even more frightening than ever, if on the whole rather more boring. The truth is I've got very tired of the utter *narrowness* of so much avant-garde music, and of the views of so many of its propagators. Composers like, say, Penderecki and Ligeti (not that they are terribly way-out, I know) seem content to go on working in such a very narrow stylistic field; I know Penderecki draws on all sorts of sources, but the end result is narrow in its application of these sources. And I admire the work of these two composers very much. So much avant-gardery seems just simply fakery, including a lot of Stockhausen, which is a pity when somebody like Stock-hausen does have a lot of music to offer but is content to do anything gimmicky that springs to his mind, presumably because he knows he can get away with it; he never seems to follow up promising ideas in his good pieces (Gruppen, Tele-musik, the piano works) or even good bits in works that otherwise don't come off (Mixtur, Hymnen). The end result is that so much of his stuff now seems to me so utterly unimaginative in any real creative sense that I just can't be bothered wading through it in the hope that 5% of it will turn out to be worthwhile; why should he carry out his experiments on me, or why should I let him when there is so much other music that is properly worked out to get to know? In short I'm getting tired of the whole avant-garde scene. So are quite a few people, I suspect; there certainly seems to be some kind of reaction against it and towards more coherent music-making. I'm not talking stylistically, but simply that I think we are moving away from the era of anything goes, though you may not think so to judge from some of the critics! […] Forgive these moans, but at times I do despair of the stranglehold fashion has on the people in power; I must admit that I seem to be doing very well despite that, but the fact remains what the audience and performers think of music seems to be the only thing those in power usually disregard, and this seems to me to be against the basic use of music.

I'm supposed to be reviewing Boulez's book, so your comments will come in very useful when I get down to it properly. Since he was recently interviewed in America and was quoted as saying that he wouldn't conduct the music of "bour-geois consolidators" like Brahms, Tchaikovsky and Ravel (preferring innovators like Beethoven, Berlioz, Schönberg, which seems to me too pat a distinction anyway) an event swiftly followed by the USA release of his record of popular works by Ravel, I tend to be suspicious of any public pronouncement by Boulez, I must admit! The book looks terrifying; but perhaps it should go to someone better at maths than I.

I'm not entirely surprised you remember more of Notturni than of S2; whether you like them or not, the songs are more immediately memorable, I think, and have a certain pictorial vividness which, connected with the words, certainly leave some impression. The Symphony is less direct in themes, too, but I hope you will continue to enjoy it; [...] The possibility of these two works being recorded by EMI still exists [...] They are both being done at the Festival Hall in the next months, S2 in March and Notturni (with Haitink this time) in May. [...]

I've been working extremely hard, and have got rather run-down, mainly because in the period of just over 3 weeks from Christmas I wrote a film score and did a week's concerts abroad! The film is a Hammer film called "Fear in the Night", not quite a horror film but rather a thriller, not bad at all if not earth-shaking, and I enjoyed doing the music; I don't want to do too many films, but one occasionally would be jolly good, I think, and since everybody seemed pleased with my work on this one I should be asked back some time. It will certainly mean that financially I'm at least on an even keel at last; my last bank balance was completely in the black, for the first time for more than 3 years.

[...] I'm going to Ireland in June to play a Walton concert; I'm sure actually that it will be cancelled for political reasons, but am hoping it won't. [...]

John did reviewing and articles for Records & Recording magazine, and was regarded as the reviewer for contemporary music (as well as Russian music) so his exposure to contemporary music was very considerable, quite apart from that which he heard or performed in concert.

23

To George Odam
February 26 1972
(Typed)

Southall

Many thanks for your letter. I'm delighted you enjoyed the clarinet trio, which I missed (because I forgot about it; how blasé can you get?), but I think it is one of my better pieces, and to have confirmation from a source whose opinion I value is heartening! I quite agree about a world devoted to the sound of a donkey's arse; but things are changing I think, and before long I suspect that music will be back in favour. Your remarks about percussion I can understand, though I don't agree with them; to me, the percussion department is an essential part of the make-up of the whole work, affecting even the thematic material, and as time goes on this becomes more integrated with the whole piece than before, or at least that's the way I feel when I'm writing. In any case, and I'm not really on the defensive, I don't see any real harm if one enjoys watching the orchestra; I'm quite sure that for some people my music wouldn't be half as worthwhile if they didn't enjoy watching the percussionists wandering about and hitting things, because for many people I'm sure the actual content of the music is still too far out for them to follow it purely by ear. Not that I'm far out really, but for many people I'm very modern, and I think it helps them to see the percussion and enjoy the physical antics. That's not why I use percussion, of course, but I don't think it is necessarily an objection to their use; you might just as well object to the presence of a conductor because he distracts the attention, and from there on we go to the presence of the orchestra itself…

In other words, I don't think distraction of the kind you complain of matters too much; and in the case of both Notturni and the 2nd Symphony I'm quite sure that neither piece would work at all without the percussion, because they are essential to me in terms of the actual content of the music. Although the thematic structure of my music is usually a little more complex than it sounds, I do still use texture very much as a formal element, and equally if something will go on an oboe rather than, say, a xylophone, then I do use the oboe. I try to get the exact sound for what I want to express (& I think percussion can have a tremendously intensifying effect emotionally), and I shall keep on using large amounts of kitchen when I want, so there! […]

Notturni was done in Manchester this week (a Sheffield concert was cancelled because of power cuts), and went very well; I also had the pleasure of finally seeing my piece for harpsichord and orchestra get off the ground in Liverpool last Saturday, though in the event I had to play the solo myself. I enjoyed doing so, though I only had 3 hours practice and a rehearsal and then on with the show and I haven't played a harpsichord for 4 or 5 years and never solo, and am thinking of taking it up as a career; there's nothing like starting at the top.

Your remarks about Tippett's percussion writing are interesting, by the way; I must say I've felt inclined to agree sometimes, but I did find "Songs for Dov" absolutely marvellous. I have a disc of "The Vision of St. Augustine" to review, which should be absolutely fascinating; I think this is one of his finest pieces, and Monica is absolutely crazy about the work, so we should have a fine time listening to it. […]

I actually worked with Bob Auger, the sound engineer for the recording, which is how I got to know the piece. Incidentally, for those who don't know, the percussion section of the orchestra is often called the 'kitchen department' by the players.

1974–1979

24

To David Sternbach
3.1.74
(Typed)

Southall

Covered with guilt, gilt, and shame, I have to confess that I lost your last letter to me almost immediately after receiving it; I've only just now recovered it, carefully tucked away with two others of yours which I don't seem to have answered either […] I am still here, as you see, coping with my ever-growing fame and wealth; […] All right, then, lack of growing fame and immensity of growing poverty. Actually I'm doing quite well at the moment; some records have just come out here, one of some orchestral music and one of some Haydn piano sonatas, both receiving good reviews and being picked out as among the year's best records […] There are various other piano records coming out eventually, so before long I should be able to move back into the house from the garden shed and kick the police out.

In my last letter (last August; what am I doing, replying within a year?) you mentioned that I'd mentioned to you, if you are still with me, that I might be coming over to the States. Well, I came and went; had I not lost your letter I'd have got in touch, especially since by USA standards I reckon to have been not all that far away. But the itinerary was pretty tough: Nov. 5-9 inclusive at Pennsylvania State University (State College), 11 Hamilton, Ontario, 14 Kalamazoo, […] 15 Guelph, Ontario (2 mid-day concerts, which entailed leaving Kalamazoo after the reception after the evening concert, travelling by car to near Detroit airport, arriving at hotel at 3am, and leaving again at 6.30am to catch the plane to Toronto, where met by car & taken to Guelph with an hour to spare before concerts). […]

I came over with Ifor James (you must learn to spell that with an f; as in Ifor Fames (or Jamef) and we enjoyed it all very much. We were becalmed in Pittsburgh, as a matter of fact, one night, having missed our connection from Philipsburgh to Toronto owing to a snowstorm in Phil/burgh; but we simply stayed in airport hotel at colossal expense to airline, and of course I didn't have your number and by the time we were settled in I was too flaked out to do anything anyway. […]

Most of these events were simply concerts. However, there were also some lecture-recitals, master-classes and seminars. There was also a 'Horn Fandango' with Ifor, which ended with the Evening Hymn from Hansel and Gretel played by a choir of 76 horns.

[…] fantastic sound which will haunt me to my dying day and maybe longer […] I also did a lecture to the, wait for it, Comparative Literature Luncheon Group on 'The problems of transposing literary works into musical terms', no less, thereby making my international intellectual debut as British Overland Cliché Champion of 1837.

[…] I'm very keen to do some work on the Haydn piano sonatas; I'm writing a full-length book on them, and recording some of them (not, as yet, the complete set) and play them every chance I get, so am becoming a bit of a specialist and bore on the subject; […]

The 'full-length book' on Haydn Piano Sonatas turned out to be, in the end, a very slim volume, one in the series put out at that time by the BBC, entitled Music Guides. John played many concerts with the brilliant horn-player Ifor James, and wrote three horn and piano works for the pair of them.

From Peter Goodchild
January 24th 1974
(Typed)

Decca Record Company Ltd.,
9, Albert Embankment,
London.

We would certainly be interested in considering the project which you described in your letter, since as you say Haydn is becoming very much a Decca composer. I wonder whether you could arrange for me to get a copy of the EMI disc […] I think I should say at this point, although of course we will go over this ground in any subsequent discussions, that basically our interest would be more in the whole project than in any one or two recordings […]

26

From Monica to Peter Goodchild
January 30th 1974
(Typed)

Southall

[…] I'm delighted that you are interested in the project that I suggested to you regarding the Haydn Piano Sonatas, and I enclose a copy of the EMI disc for you to listen to. […] Naturally John and I are very pleased that you are thinking in terms of an entire project, rather than just one or two recordings, for this is very much what John has been hoping to do anyway. […]

This was the start of the complete Haydn solo piano music project, issued on LP by Decca in the mid to late 1970s, and still available as a CD box set after nearly 50 years. Decca was recording many complete Haydn cycles at the time, including symphonies, string quartets and piano trios.

27

From William Alwyn
Oct. 7 1975
(Hand-written)

Lark Rise,
Blythburgh,
Halesworth,
Suffolk.

Richard Butt, from the BBC Birmingham, who is an old friend of ours, came here last week to record an interview with me for "Portrait of the Composer", which is being broadcast near my birthday. He was so surprised when I spoke of my debt to you in this interview ('an older composer surely *never* admits that he is indebted to a younger one!') that a day or two after he sent me as a gift the record of your "Notturni ed Alba" & 2nd Symphony. I only had time to play the "Notturni" once, as the following day I had to go up to London (I've just got back) to, of all things, give a talk to the Elgar Society on Elgar as a conductor (having of course many times played under Elgar's baton in the LSO). This is to tell you what a very <u>beautiful</u> work it is, and how much I loved it. Your complete mastery of orchestration! I'm always chary of percussion as you've probably noticed in my own works (I find Ben Britten's "Death in Venice" far too indulgent in this respect) , but your exquisite use of percussion in the "Notturni" has converted me – though, for myself, I expect I shall still treat them with caution. Also I think Richard wanted me to hear Jill Gomez's performance, as the BBC are trying to get her to play the name part in my new opera , "Miss Julie", next year. […]

28

From William Alwyn
Nov. 9 1975
(Hand-written)

Blythburgh

How very delightful of you to think of my 70th and to send me not only your good wishes, but two records. [...] "The Chagall Windows" is a magnificent symphonic work – wholly satisfying shape and masterly in execution, with passages of great beauty. This is a piece which will surely remain in the repertoire. I liked the Hartmann Variations though I do think that the only excuse for using variations form is symphonically (in continual evolution) as in the "Windows", and of course they were overshadowed by the later work. [...]

William Alwyn wrote frequently to John in the 1970s and up to the mid-1980s. He had felt very neglected and snubbed during the period of fashionable avant-garde music. John, writing in Records & Recording had highly praised Alwyn's Third and Fifth Symphonies, for which Alwyn felt much gratitude, leading to a long correspondence between the two composers.

29

To The Times
28.4.76
(Typed)

Southall

The philosophy of Mr Williams (April 26) appears to be that no-one should be obliged to contribute money to anything from which they do not personally benefit. He is obviously insensible to the essential contribution made by the arts to the quality of life in general. The *minute* amount every citizen pays towards the arts in a year (far less than I contribute as a self-employed person to unemployment and sick benefits which I am not entitled to draw upon) goes towards enriching the life of the community at large, by spreading the availability of the arts at a realistic personal cost to any member of society who wishes to experience them.

It is dismaying to find this correspondence propagating familiar myths about music. The conductor's fee, large or small, is merely one among many costs involved in concert-giving – were ticket prices to reflect these costs without public subsidy, few people would be able to afford to attend concerts, to say nothing of opera or ballet, and the art would simply die. Further, I strongly deprecate the view that classical music is for the "intelligentsia" alone. Perhaps a snobbish group of music-lovers would like it to remain their own private preserve. Conversely there are others who use "intelligentsia" or some other class-induced word as an excuse for their own lack of interest. For me, as for most musicians, music is music and appeals to whoever has ears to hear it. It should be added that the view of classical music as a tiny minority interest is utterly untrue – the vast audience for it testifies to its lasting power to move and involve people.

There had been a lengthy correspondence in The Times on the topic of conductors' fees, I think centred around a fee for Georg Solti. The final word belonged to John. The phrase "Music is music" meaning to him that he made no distinction between the best of any variety of music, is one that he used throughout his life, and most movingly at the end. Sadly, however, currently many pressures militate against the performance and dissemination of classical music.

30

From Harold Truscott
12/12/76
(Typed)

School of Music,
The Polytechnic,
Huddersfield, HD1 3DH,
Yorks.

[…] I thoroughly enjoyed your concert last Thursday, and also seeing you and being able to talk to you. I wish it was possible to see you more often and talk more […] Incidentally, you may be interested, if you are able to listen, in a talk I recorded a few months ago, on Bantock, which is being broadcast next Sunday […] Also his marvellous symphony for unaccompanied choir, Atalanta in Calydon, is being recorded […] for future broadcast.'

Harold Truscott, writer and composer, had wide-ranging knowledge and sympathies, but John did not in the end take up his piano sonatas, proffered in this letter.

31

To Monica McCabe
Dated only Sunday night, but c. 22/23 February 1977
(Hand-written)

Midland Hotel,
Peter Street,
Manchester,
2M60 2DS.

Having been rude on the phone, I thought it would be nice if I dropped you a line before I got to bed! I've just finished my list of music pieces for the film, & there are 9 bits of music & 5 of the "noise", which is a good deal better than the total of 24! The problem is going to be that they all <u>talk</u> so much, & get very het up if somebody else is talking at the same time. Also <u>Sir</u> gets very muddled at times & rabbits on about something we haven't got to yet, which leads to a lengthy bout of confusion all round. I think I'll have to be ready to say something about not wanting to go into overtime on Tuesday! They're going to have a video-cassette machine at the recording session, which is fine, except they won't be able to use it because by the time they've found the right bit of film we'll be rehearsing the next bit of music. That really might be a problem.

Still, it will be most interesting to see how it turns out – I hope the nervous strain is worth it! It will be nice to get home & relax, even if I do have to do some re-writing of the Piano Concerto for Ilan as soon as I get back. But after this week, please God I will have a bit of time to stop and think. There are times when, however entertaining the disasters may be, they do get on top of one!

The film in question was 'Come back, little Sheba', starring Joanne Woodward, Carrie Fisher and Sir Laurence Olivier, and John found 'Sir' very irritating indeed. Olivier insisted on knowing more about music than John did (though he had of course worked with Walton). I don't recall what rudeness, if any, John had shown me – perhaps my call had interrupted one of those edgy conferences. He was in fact very tired, having only just got back from a frenetic visit to the United States in time to deal with this film. Despite Olivier's exasperating behaviour his performance in the film was superb. 'Ilan' was Ilan Rogoff, for whom John was writing his Third Piano Concerto.

32

From Peter Racine Fricker
September 25 1977
(Typed)

5423 Throne Court,
Santa Barbara,
California 93111.

[…] I'm glad to be able to send you my thanks for the recording of the cello sonata (I must write to Julian too). I've only just got the record; it doesn't seem to be available here yet […] A strong and lively performance, and I'm very pleased. I liked your work very much, and I will introduce it to our cellist […] And I must also thank you for the fine performance of the Horn Sonata with Ifor James. I don't have an address for him, so perhaps you would convey my gratitude to him. Incidentally, I ordered some records a short time ago, among them one of you playing your own works.

Fricker had long been domiciled in California. His star has currently dimmed in Britain, but both the cello and the horn sonata are strong works.

33

To Barney Childs
January 11ᵗʰ 1978
(Typed)

Southall

New Year Greetings from us both! Life here is extremely hectic, which is why I haven't been in touch before. However, in regard to my forthcoming visit to Redlands, there are a few points I'd like to clear up if possible. First, I enclose some photos of me, plus biography […] You will notice that I now have a beard, the result of an attack of chicken-pox last autumn, since I was unable to shave for a while and rather like the beard that grew as a result (and to which I am, of course, deeply attached). […] We've agreed programme and dates for piano recital and piano master-class on Haydn, May 11-14 inclusive. I haven't heard anything […] regarding the new band piece […] I'd be grateful for this to be confirmed, as I expect to write the score of it as soon as possible and would hate to do the work on it and then find it had been cancelled! The title, by the way, is Images and it lasts c. 14 mins.

The other thing which needs to be tied up is the suggestion of the Anderson Living-Learning Centre, where you suggested I might stay and thus be available to students for onformal [sic] chats at odd times [...] I always enjoy chatting to students on an informal basis, and I'm quite ready to do what I can in this direction during my stay. [...]

The symphonic wind band version of Images was premiered May 14th 1978 in Redlands, California. The composer Barney Childs was to become a close friend of John's, with whom he frequently stayed while in the US.

34

From Don Banks
4 Mar 78
(Typed – badly)

c/o Australia Music Centre Ltd.,
PO Box N9, Grosvenor St.,
Sydney, NSW 2000.

Dear Sir or Madam,

I have just returned to "home base" after 2 hectic weeks on the road for a Composers/Performers Seminar in Melbourne followed by appearances at the Adelaide Festival with ACME (Australian Contemporary Music Ensemble) which – following my usual stupid penchant for setting up new things – has achieved beyond my wildest etc. I PRAY FOR A BAD REVIEW! [...] H*O*W*E*V*E*R the news is that I have resigned from the Canberra School of Music but pushed hard for your visit there with X luck but am now HEAD OF THE SCHOOL OF COMPOSITION STUDIES at the N.S.W. State Cons. Of Music, as from 17th Feb. where one of my first duties was to approve of a lecture by your good-self (I had to explain our usual arrangement whereby the cheque is made payable to me and I give you 5% - OK). A WORD OF WARNING SPORT: You'll find that the ABC here tend to say "we're a small country – little dissemination of material – so as PR for you we'll record and tape you and make you known here – so please waive all broadcast fees! Don't fall for it. [...]

Adelaide Festival was a gas. ACME won accolades like mad. Like Jane Manning wants to return in November to record the Webern songs and said Keith Humble was so superior to Boulez [...] R.R. Bennet [sic] reckons ACME is one of the best chamber ensembles he has heard. [...] Mr Bowen protected Sir MT so well I never saw him. Oscar Peterson and Joe Pass were a gas [...] Thanks for your thoughts about my music John – I think you'd like my recent piece "4x2x1x" for 2 clarients [sic] 1 player and computer tape (oh yes, my dear, we do try to keep up with technology. Actually I'm a fake. I sit at the computer which can give me "real-time" sounds – look impressive punching in via tele-type instructions for hexi-decimal, octal and binary instructions etc., and just using my ears for the sounds I want. Know of any other method???????? Mind you, it took me FIVE F.....G MONTHS to learn to talk to the computer [...] DARLING MONICA; I LOVE YOU MADLY AND AM SO PLEASED YOU'VE PASSED YOUR DRIVING TEST. [...]

Do write.

1.30 am: no cricket: I've had it. Let the Windies trash our 3rd team and see if I care. The Packer series has been great. Camera coverage fantastic. They had to take out the buried mikes close to the batsmen owing to their filthy language. But really, their repartee would have made Warren Mitchell blush (who I was glad to meet here 3 nights ago in Adelaide) and his [...] talk is bad enough even for us pure living Australian types [...]

This letter has been slightly censored for idiomatic Australian. Don Banks was a wild man Aussie jazz, classical and film composer, and very highly gifted, as well as very funny. He died, sadly, much too young, at the age of 57. John thought very highly of him and his music. Warren Mitchell starred as the foul-mouthed racist bigot in the ground-breaking BBC TV comedy series 'Till Death Us Do Part'.

35

From David Maslanka
8/5/78
(Hand-written)

No address

Thanks for your most cordial letter. Separate package is a copy of PIANO SONG. As you will discover, the piece is deceptively simple. It requires precise timing, a resonant and responsive piano (a resonant and responsive audience!) and a warm hall. I do hope the work will satisfy you and be of use to you. The clarinet pieces will be sent before long. Barney [*Childs*] and Phil [*Rehfeldt*] are now in the process of recording them for CRI. Yes, they are very tricky! I have also just completed a three-movement piece for cello and piano, with which I am very pleased. I will let you have a copy.

Barney <u>is</u> a most extraordinary person – he has been both friend and mentor – has helped me through some very difficult stretches of my life. I most appreciate his clarity of thought and insight and his tough-mindedness. Rare qualities. [...]

technique – after all, even John Christian said he wouldn't care to attempt Clementi in public […]

Charles Cudworth was the curator of the Pendlebury Music Library in Cambridge, and a dear friend of mine. John was taking a big interest in Clementi's piano sonatas at this time and went on to record a selection, still available on a Divine Art CD. Charles's particular enthusiasm was for music around the period of J.C. Bach. He himself altered the year on this letter, which makes it rather unclear. It may belong to 1976 or 1977, rather than 1978.

41

From Nicholas Maw
December 4th 1978
(Typed)

92, Priory Road,
London NW6 3NL.

Many thanks for your note. And many more thanks for playing Personae in York. I'm truly sorry that you were obliged to play them under such duress, and can only hope the headache was not caused by the pieces! […] I have no doubt your playing of them does them more than justice, headache or no headache. I'm delighted to hear you will be doing them at the Wigmore in January […] I have not forgotten I promised you another one, and I can assure you that I will try to get down to it the moment I have the opportunity. I will try to tailor it to your playing. […] Booseys are supposedly starting work on the publication of the first three, so hopefully you will not have to struggle with my MS for ever.

I was very impressed with a broadcast a few weeks back of a concert you did earlier this year from – I think – Boston, Lincs. of the Haydn F minor Variations, Schumann Op. 4 and your own Liszt Fantasia [*sic*]. In a sense I knew what to expect with the Haydn and also with your playing of your own music (the Fantasia seems to me a highly successful concert work which should be in the repertoire of any discerning pianist – are there any?), but I was particularly struck by your playing of the Schumann (a marvellous work) which I have never heard you play before, and with whom you seem to have a real affinity. You seemed to play it as if you had written it yourself – and no higher compliment can I give! […]

42

To Nicholas Maw
12th December 1978
(Typed)

Southall

[…] I shall look forward eagerly to the fourth Personae (or should that be Persona?) but really I do intend to have a go at number 3 eventually. By the way, regarding number 2, what is the last note? I remember when I played the piece through to you there was some doubt about it…..in my copy it is a B, but I noticed in the example printed in the recent article in Tempo it was written as a C. I played a C in York, and personally don't like it as much as B.

John played Personae I and II in York, a live concert recorded by the BBC. He travelled from London to York by train, and developed a headache by the time of the concert. He did tackle Personae III eventually. Regarding II, he has pencilled (B) on his two copies of the music. Nicholas did eventually write Personae IV, V and VI, published in 1985 and performed by Peter Donohoe in Bath. However, I don't believe that IV was written for John. Nicholas might not have been remiss in this. Very possibly the commission was for Donohoe to give the premiere.

43

From Richard Rodney Bennett
Undated, but probably early 1979
(Hand-written)

45 W 54th # 9E
NYC,
NY 10019

I was sorry to miss you when I was in London; a brief phone-message was not enough to thank you for the good flute pieces […] I was very touched by your reaction to Sonnets to Orpheus. It was a piece I urgently wanted to write & I think it was wonderfully well played; for once I didn't get my usual reviews – facile, the usual lovely sounds (ugh!), no depth etc. Even a critic in the Irish Gazette (or something) said it was the most boring 45 mins. of his entire life, which is at least dramatic.

I've never been happier than living in New York & have never worked harder. I even have a busy social life here, which is a lot of fun. My social life in London narrowed itself down to the occasional trip to the Screen on the Green or an

Indian restaurant (the only thing I miss here) [...] I've done a ballet about the crazed Isadora Duncan; I always wanted to write music about sex but by the end of the second & last act, which is almost uninterrupted copulation, I had so to speak worked <u>that</u> out of my system.....Now I have to cope with 2 pieces both of which I thought I wanted to write (string octet and chamber orch.) but have discovered now that the crunch has come, that I have no interest in at all. The only thing I want to do is the piece <u>after</u> that – amplified harpsichd. (yet) & orch.

By the way I think the mi. 3rd similarity at the beginning of Sonnets to O. & the 3rd Szymanowski (or as a friend of mine determinedly & endearingly refers to him – Syzmanowski) is perfectly splendid and sensible; major 3rds too cozy & maj. & mi. 2nds boring. [...]

One of the things I like most about being here is that I have nothing <u>whatever</u> to do with the classical music establishment, apart from the dear Thea [Musgrave], & another close composer friend. It is so nice not to be involved in all those squabbles & committees. When Jane Manning was here and talked uninterruptedly for 4 days about Ollie Knussen (about whom I have a good deal to say but refrain from doing so) I nearly lost my reason. I need scores & records & some contact with certain composers, hence this letter, but that is that.

By the way, under no circumstances have anything to do with a slim vol. by Charles Wuorinen, rather disingenuously called Simple Composition; it is all about combinatoriality, the time-point system, modules, dyads and what seems to me to be higher mathematics. It makes me want to give up the <u>whole</u> business.

I heard a RAVISHING new orch. piece by Lutoslawski in Washington. It is called Novelette, which I think is a mistake as it suggest Women's Own & Ethel M. Dell, but it sounds wonderful. I wish I could write all those whirling notes but can't & will just keep writing tunes.

Despite the above, Richard was, or became, a close friend of Wuorinen. He had a duo with Jane Manning, which he later passed to John when he went to live in New York. Jane was a genius, and a lovely, warm-hearted, generous person, but could pack more words into a minute than anyone I ever knew. Tony Payne the composer, her husband, would occasionally interject, 'Shut up, Jane', which she always took in good part. The flute pieces were a contribution to a Novellos series of teaching works, under Richard's general editorship. In this letter, Richard seems to display the beginnings of a later disillusionment with contemporary music.

44

From Robert Simpson
9.V.79
(Hand written)

Yalding House
156 Great Portland Street,
London W1N 6AJ.

As promised, here's a copy of Nielsen's letter about the pfte. Variations – it's only a rough translation, by a chap who's done the whole volume. He proposes to try & get them published, but they need polishing first. It's a revealing letter, I think.

About the programmes – I'd be more than grateful if you'd do the Chaconne and the Pieces for Young & Old (both books) (in different programmes) and I'll use Arne's recording of the Variations, the big Suite and the three late pieces. If you're happy about this I'll send you bookings – that means I'll have the piano music shared by the 2 best Nielsen players!

John accepted this, though I'm sure he would have liked to have done the big Suite himself. 'Arne' would be Arne Skjold Rasmussen, a notable Nielsen pianist.

45

To David Sternbach
June 6th 1979
(Typed)

Southall

[…] I do apologise, as we say over here, for not writing sooner, but as you will see ere long this has been a difficult year, full of action, inaction, disaction, dataction, and so forth. […]

I've caught up on composition, and we've actually had a short holiday in the Lake District, where for 4/10ths of the time the sun was either visible or almost visible […]

At the moment it's piano time again, and as usual I have far too many works to play in a short period of time. I'm also doing research into the piano sonatas (three of which I have and which are splendid) of one George Frederick Pinto, who dies [*sic*] in 1806 at the age of 21 as a result of 'excesses'. Pinto was his mother's name; his father was called Sanders, and I suspect was a Kentucky Colonel. Anyway the sonatas (which are not available in print) that I've got are fascinating, and I'm now trying to add to my burdens by hunting the remaining four to see if they are as good […]

These are short sections from a long letter to his friend David, who has enquired about the possibilities of moving to work in Britain. John points out the difficulties, including the need to live here for a year before being able to join the Musicians' Union, essential for any orchestral or session work. John has also had a number of health problems, while his mother has suffered a heart attack, but survived. For those who know nothing about the gastronomic delight, Kentucky Fried Chicken, it was a Colonel Sanders who supposedly set up its world-wide distribution.

46

From David Willcocks
13. vi. 1979
(Typed)

Royal College of Music,
Prince Consort Road,
South Kensington,
London SW7 2BS.

I have consulted the Keeper of the Parry Room Library concerning our holdings of piano sonatas of G.F. Pinto and he informs me that we possess Op. 3 Nos. 1 & 2 (Eb minor and A major which you already have) Op. 4 Nos. 1, 2, & 3 (G, Bb, C).

We do not possess the C minor sonata.

Dr. Watkins Shaw points out that the three works in Op. 4 are slight Sonatini-type compositions including such things as a Waltz, March, Irish Air, and are not comparable to the E flat minor, A major or C minor works. He felt that you might like to know this fact (or alternatively come in to look at them) before deciding on Xeroxing 24 pages at 10p each plus packing and postage.

Why not come and have lunch one day when you are near?

From Harold Truscott
7/7/79
(Hand-written)

16, Claremont Rd.,
Deal,
Kent.

Here are photocopies of Clementi's Op. 50, Nos. 1 & 2. At least, you can see from these what they are like, and I hope you like them. The slow movement of the D minor is closely connected in style with that of "Didone Abbandonata"; it's curious how often he used this slow 6/8 approach in his middle and later sonatas: the slow movement of the G minor, Op. 34, No. 2, the large opening introduction to the B minor, Op. 40, No. 2, and the slow passage between the quick movements of the same sonata, the slow movement of the D major, Op. 40 No. 3, and the major part of the large opening introduction to the E minor Caprice Sonata. I suppose, too, the 5/4 Adagio introduction of the C major Caprice Sonata is related, too, with its slow moving quaver triplets.

David Willcocks was of course the Principal of the Royal College of Music in London, as well as a distinguished choral conductor. John continued to explore repertoire all his life. He was very taken with both the Pinto and the Clementi sonatas, performing them on numerous occasions in recital. He also recorded three Clementi sonatas, including the best-known 'Didone Abbandonata' for Hyperion, now available on a Divine Art CD. A recording of three Pinto sonatas was never issued, because of the poor sound quality of the recording. Harold Truscott was helpful to John in the matter of the music of both Pinto and Clementi.

MIDDLE EAST TOUR CORRESPONDENCE

From John to Monica

October/November 1979

During these two months John undertook a lengthy tour throughout the Middle East, giving about 14 recitals and also lectures and master-classes, on behalf of the British Council. The political situation in the Middle East was already very troubled. The Shah of Iran had been deposed in February 1979, and the so-called Islamic Revolution had taken place. A peace treaty had been signed between Israel and Egypt, but there were many tensions especially in Egypt. John had paid a previous visit to Israel, for the Granada TV film about his orchestral work, The Chagall Windows. Because of this he had to have a new passport specially prepared without the Israel stamp, and for some time he actually had two pass-ports. The travel was gruelling, especially as apart from his own personal needs of clothes and music etc, he had to take with him an enormous and heavy British Council suitcase full of their promotional material. Some tour changes were made at the very last minute, because of political unrest. In the end his tour took him to Ankara, Riyadh, Jeddah, Baghdad, Kuwait, Damascus, Amman, and then to Belgrade, Varadzin, Zagreb and Novi Sad. His visit to Egypt was cancelled. Lebanon was also very troubled at that time. The inclusion of the Eastern European venues meant that he had to take warmer clothes as well as lighter ones. I no longer have his original itinerary, but in any case changes were made at the last minute, or even en route. A postcard announces his safe arrival in Ankara. His following letters are typed, but largely undated, except for days of the week.

48

Riyadh

Wednesday

Well, here I am, waiting for the second concert of the tour, and of course feeling very nervous, but things seem to have gone pretty well so far [...] I'm enjoying myself seeing the places and meeting people; the pianos are a little worse than we feared (can't use the soft pedal because of a Great Squak – that should be Squeak, but I actually quite like it); the people all very helpful. I've been extremely well looked after, both here and in Ankara, and have had some washing done here too.

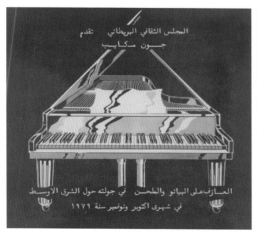

Front and Back Covers for John's British Council tour of the Middle East, in English and Arabic, 1979. **48**

It started very well; as you recall, with BA not making any comment about the excess baggage. Undoubtedly this was because they must have seen that I was the sort of person likely to be carrying a credit note for this, because when we got to Istanbul and transferred all my luggage to the other terminal [...] they of course demanded money. What with getting porters, a taxi between terminals, and this, I've used up most of my small denomination dollars [...]

Eager hands clutch your luggage at every airport, & you're likely to find yourself pursuing a porter a long way ahead of you unless you're careful & shake your head with great frequency. Needless to say there was a mix-up at Istanbul [...] Fortunately it all worked out OK. I was at a hotel, quite a good one, and had dinner out, and Monday was quite frantic. The morning was taken up with getting a Saudi Arabian visa [...] then there was a lunch to meet a few local musicians [...]

Handbill for John's Riyadh recital, the first ever given before a mixed audience of men and women, 1979. **48**

then practising, then changing, quick visits to two cocktail parties (no, I didn't drink) [...] then the concert, then dinner with various notables. I think I coped pretty well with all this, but it was a hell of a day [...] Ankara was in a small hall, but it filled to over-flowing – tonight's is in a massive hotel banqueting hall, the most sumptuous modern thing that money could build, and it should be very nice; tonight's is the first public recital ever held in a public place with a mixed audience (men & women) and we still haven't got formal approval for this. There's really too much to tell you in so short a letter [...] because in a couple of minutes I must start getting ready for the concert [...] .a pity that conditions here are really not conducive to keeping pianos [...]

49

Jeddah (Djidda)
18. 10. 79

Botschaft der Bundesrepublik Deutschland

As you see, German Embassy notepaper. I am ensconced in a splendid private suite, & awaiting news of what I'm going to do tomorrow, or what I'm going to be allowed to do [...]

No complaints about Ankara or Riyadh, though. At Ankara, as I said, I was well looked after & although given too much to do in 1 day I did it – all part of the job. Riyadh was the place, though – I can now tell you, we were all mightily relieved that it went very well. An audience of over 400, and we weren't raided, which was a distant prospect... [...] But despite a piano on which I was unable to use the soft pedal [...] it went extremely well, and the people there seemed delighted. I felt really moved by the warmth of the sentiments expressed to me afterwards, & it was of course a genuine historic occasion [...] When I tell you that John Ewart, my host, wanted to take me into a museum & couldn't because until noon it was only open to ladies, that will give you an idea of the basic rules. Europeans are expected to abide by the rules, though in the privacy of their own homes they are allowed to do what they like as long as it is discreet. This seems to me perfectly fair, & actually very sensible.

In Riyadh, apart from playing in the most sumptuous hall imaginable, I took tea with the high official who was responsible for giving us verbal permission to hold the concert – this was very much an audience, with various sheikhs sitting round drinking tea and coffee & being summoned by the sheikh we had all come to see. At the concert hall [...] my green-room was the King's private suite for use during Conferences held at the hotel [...] gold-plated taps and wash-basins. This morning I went for a drive to Diriyadh, the previous capital (Riyadh is the new one, & when I say new, most of it has been built in the last 10 years). The ruins of this are most evocative, & it's rather a pity that in the town concrete, albeit of a high quality [...] is replacing the old wattle-and-daub type of material, because this has great charm of texture. But the new architecture, like the old, is extremely beautiful, with a wonderful variety of exotic shapes but never overpowering. The colours are predominantly a kind of gentle Cotswold stone colour [...] with many roofs of an emerald green, & occasionally a white house. But there's nothing glaring, & even on a hot, sunny morning like today, I found it perfectly satisfactory to go without dark glasses. [...]

Jeddah is on the coast – I haven't seen much of it, so will reserve comment. [...] Enough of this. I must go to sleep [...] and although I wouldn't have missed

this experience, I'm sorry that you are not sharing it. Though it would be difficult for you in many ways – you'd have to be careful where you went outside,
because you'd not be able to go in some places with me. I'm sure you'd <u>love</u>
the driving, as long as you didn't have to do any yourself! [...] with car-horn
tooting continuously & the wildest driving you've ever seen.

*John had originally been annoyed that he had seemingly been 'dumped' on a
foreign Embassy. However, it turned out there had been good reasons for this, to
do with family illness, and he was very well looked after at the German Embassy.
During the letter he muses about the British he has met so far, and praises those
who enter imaginatively into the spirit of the place.*

50

Probably from Baghdad
22-10-79
(Hand-written, but again on German Embassy paper)

Some more impressions while I wait for my 4th concert. My last letter is on
its way to you in the Diplomatic Bag, you'll be interested to hear. I'm sorry
I can't type this, but typewriters cannot be brought into Iraq because of the
spy industry, apparently. Incidentally, there is undoubtedly a tape recording
of our phone call last night, if you understand me! Jeddah turned out a little
disappointing because of the rain, which occasioned the moving of the piano
to a drier area, & an itinerant & vociferous cat who took a fancy to the concert.
Wild cats & wild dogs roam Riyadh & Jeddah [...] A lot of Riyadh in particular
is being demolished & new buildings being put up, & there are heaps of rubble
& rubbish from time to time, infested with these packs of wild animals.

Baghdad is a strange place. A lot of it is modern, but there are a number of
beautiful-looking mosques, & the drive across the city (& across the Tigris river,
which I've crossed 4 times now, I think – remember the Tigris & Euphrates
from your schooldays?) goes through an old part (the souk, presumably [...])
which is completely different. There is so much dust & earth in the narrow side-
streets that in this part it covers the tarmac roads with a fine layer of earth. The
smell is like a combination of rotten eggs & some fairly exotic spice [...]

I was given 1 and a half hours in the Iraq Museum this morning – very tiring,
of course, but very interesting. A lot of splendid circular seals, which depict
all kinds of things but are particularly worthwhile because they include many
scenes of ordinary life as lived all those years ago. Also saw the original of the
Royal Game of Ur! Postcard collecting not terribly easy, but I had bought for me

a number of some fine objects at the museum. The piano is a Grotrian-Steinweg, reasonable, though I fancy it will go out of tune as the concert progresses. [...]

Lots of sirens zooming down the main road, & earlier a lot of shouting & a few people running – I hope no trouble! The lecture tomorrow <u>may</u>, if the piano's good enough, be piano music by RRB, Maw and me [...] By the way, I left my raincoat in Riyadh. It will, I hope, be returned in the Diplomatic Bag. [...]

John also spoke again of the disappointment of the small size of the audience in Jeddah. However, rather bad planning had made this coincide with the great Hajj pilgrimage. RRB was of course Richard Rodney Bennett. The visit to the Iraq Museum is both interesting and sad. I believe that this was the museum which was so badly wrecked and looted of many antiquities during the Iraq War. The original of the Royal Game of Ur was of interest to us, because John had given me a set of this antique board game, bought I believe in the Metropolitan Museum in New York.

51

Kuwait
Wednesday

British Reps. Residence,
Kuwait.

I have now arrived in Kuwait and in fact arrived last night, after an extremely eventful day [...]

The Baghdad concert went extremely well – the best audience they've had in that hall, which was attached to a very pleasant library. A good number of Iraqis among the 300 or so audience, and I was presented with an absolutely superb spread of flowers before playing the encore. I was also, incidentally, presented with a heavy book after my concert in Riyadh, a book that I rather wanted to get anyway. [...]

Both clasps have now fallen off the British Council suitcase, which is but a shadow of its former self. It got badly beaten up on the plane to Jeddah, which was a jumbo packed with pilgrims going to Mecca [...] and has sustained various cuts and abrasions on its travels. If I can possibly get everything left after here into the holdall and the black suitcase, I will leave the BC one here. [...] The Rep here is a keen music-lover and record fan [...]

Residencies: all the British Council reps live in very spacious houses, this one being the finest. I have the whole top floor to myself [...] beautifully furnished throughout. Every house has a servant who comes and does cleaning, cooking, laundry etc, and I'm hoping to leave here with my clothes all nicely refreshed. [...] I have been looked after extremely well throughout the tour and perhaps with the greatest care so far in Riyadh [...] and Baghdad. The latter, incidentally, is a very dusty place, and there was a hint of a dust-storm at one point [...] These countries are all very different from each other, despite obvious similarities. [...]

The visit to Baghdad ended somewhat dramatically. In the morning I did my lecture, doing piano music instead of the one using the prepared tape, which is really less interesting to relatively unsophisticated students than to have someone actually talking and playing the music himself. It went very well, and seemed to be appreciated. [...] we decided I'd spend the afternoon doing some composition with perhaps a walk round the souk a bit later on and in the evening visits to two official functions. At one o'clock the bloke from the Council turned up [...] with my flight ticket saying that flight schedules had been changed [...] Kuwait Airways now said that I had been put on a flight leaving not at 9.15am but at 11pm, which would be half an hour after my concert here [Kuwait] should have ended. Panic all round. Intense discussion of possible alternatives. All offices shut until 5 in the afternoon. It was discovered there was an Iraqi Airways flight at 7, but it was felt that it would be fully booked [...]

The whole story is lengthy and complex, and at one point John expressed a willingness to be driven to the border, pass through Customs checks, and hopefully be met by another driver the other side, all of which would entail getting up at 4am, and 12 hours of car travel. The concert the next day was fully booked. Eventually, through the goodwill of British Airways, another flight was found, the problem having been one of over-booking, probably because of the Hajj. John continues:-

[...] I arrived here at 1am, with my BC suitcase disintegrating. But there was a driver here to greet me and take me to the Residence and I was given a drink and sat up until 4 chatting [...] I slept very well until 10.30 and felt lively as a cricket.

Next day: concert now over, and seemed to go pretty well. Piano not too good, but not execrable [...] Full house, as you'll have gathered – c. 300 people. Afterwards there was a reception at the house of a rich young Lebanese couple [...] I'd had a rather more disturbed tummy than usual during the day [...] and was afraid the bugs had caught up with me, but I decided to go, and not only went and enjoyed myself but ate well of excellent fascinating food [...] and am today less worried. A little bubbly inside, but better than yesterday [...] At 1am back to the residence, where conversation flowed until 4 again. Apparently the Rep has a name for staying up late, and it would be difficult if a) the conversation were not so stimulating, and b) in the next day or so I have time to rest. This morning gave my lecture, which was in the open-air in a courtyard surrounded by several floors of rooms in which crockery-throwing contests appeared to be taking place [...] My brief from London was to deal with British music, so I decided to do one hour of my piano music talk (RRB, Maw, McCabe again) [...]

From Gordon Green
15.5.80
(Hand-written)

University College Hospital,
Gower Street,
London W.C. 1.

A short note. I have not been well for some months now and it has been decided that I have lung cancer. I arrived in this hospital this afternoon and it is <u>hoped</u> that I shall be operated on on Monday. Alas this is not the end of our troubles. During the past few days dear Dorothy has become increasingly unable to maintain her balance. She has seen a neurologist and had tests; but her condition has become worse and we have had to get her into hospital also […]

Gordon Green was John's loved and admired piano-teacher, for much of his life, even as a child. He was also the teacher of many other leading and successful pianists, including John Ogdon, Stephen Hough and Philip Fowke. It was at the house of the Greens, in Liverpool, that John as a young boy made the acquaintance of Alan Rawsthorne, who was their close friend. Dorothy had been a ballet dancer in her younger days, and was an accomplished cook, who started up and ran one of Liverpool's favourite dining clubs, a Mecca for musicians, when the country opened up again after World War II. Gordon was writing from University College Hospital, London. Sadly neither Gordon nor Dorothy were to survive long.

57

To David Sternbach
Sept. 10th 1980
(Typed)

Southall

Is it really but X months since we received yours of a certain date? Yes, it is. Well, that's enough for now. […] Wait a minute, wasn't there something else? If this epistle so far has seemed a little strained (strange), harassed, crazy, this is only natural. I am at present involved in writing the music for episodes of a TV series of horror films, and the present one, which I should have finished writing yesterday, I can't start yet, because instead of taking 10 days to shoot it they took 20. 100% is a pretty good error margin, I trust you will agree. The previous one I did should have been 52 minutes long, and when with their infinite care, patience, technical skill and general stupidity they had cut it all together it lasted a mere 44 minutes, and then it was too long by half, I can tell you. Another TV company I'm doing a little tune for have decided not to inform me as to what is going on, so I can't yet write out a score until I know how many instruments I can use, like do I write it for the Philadelphia Orchestra or do I score it for piccolo and ophicleide. I have a recital in 4 days time for which I am just practising, not one piece of which occurs in my programmes for the rest of the season – good planning. I am off to Australia on 26th having the previous morning given a festival recital on [*sic*] North Wales most of the repertoire for which I am not using again for the rest of the season. People are refusing to tell me which programme they want me to play for my recitals when I get back here from Australia, and, as the final piece of good planning, I get back here on 21st October and have a recital <u>the same night</u> in London. It's a damned good thing, sir and madam (lady and madman) that I am a sane, well-balanced, psychologically orientated lunatic. [...]

This clash of engagements was not really John's fault. TV and film people always left the music till the last moment. Hammer Films was particularly bad in this respect, biking over cue sheets daily, often mistakenly the same ones as the previous day. No-one understood the need for the composer to have precise details. Extracting programme requirements from concert planners could be like pulling teeth. The Australia flight the day after a concert in North Wales was unfortunate, but many musicians' diaries read in the same way. The concert engagement for the same day as John's return from Australia was a very special event. He was taking part in a celebratory concert for the Park Lane Group. He played Haydn, and played perfectly!

58

From Robert Simpson
17 IX 80
(Typed)

Cedar Cottage,
Chearsley,
Aylesbury,
Bucks. HP18 0DA.

Thanks for your nice letter – no need to feel guilty; I know how much you have to do. I got enormous encouragement and support from all over the place, inside as well as outside the BBC. Now I can say what I like and I will. That little matter of the Proms is high on my agenda, and for a start I had the chance to refuse a commission for a symphony for next year's Proms. How could I possibly accept it from the person I think should not be there to offer it? […] Thanks for your comment on No. 6, but it was an <u>awful</u> performance and I'm amazed that anyone could have found it anything but dull. I sat there and sweated no end. I suppose you can't expect much else when they see it for the first time the day before. They did their admirable best, but could only make sure of not getting out […]

59

From John to Monica
1/10/80
(Hand-written)

Earle Page College,
Armidale,
NSW, Australia.

I'm sitting out on the grass in blazing sunshine, improving on my sun tan & feeling very well. Tonight I'm off to Inverell (not too far) for my 1st recital (evening-type) […] I can certainly say I've never been so well looked-after anywhere. Overwhelming kindness, & all directed at making things as easy as possible for me. […] The recital [Macquarie University, Sydney] itself was moderate (Nielsen a bit indiscriminate). I'm not now playing the Clementi at all, which is a pity in one way, but eases the pressure […] The flight here was pretty good […] We stopped in Bahrein & Singapore and were able to stretch our legs. A splendid electrical storm in Singapore, which believe it or not I watched with great fascination. Air travel for such a long time induces a curiously unreal psychological state, so that nothing seems true any more – otherwise I dare say I'd have been scared stiff […] Now about to be filmed, being interviewed for radio, if you follow me […]

At home, John was not a storm lover. His visits to Australia were almost invariably filled with kindness, consideration and generosity.

60

From John to Monica
5.10.80
(Hand-written)

Jimbour (?) House,
Dalby.

Jimbour House is the lovely big house which was once the main house of a huge sheep station. [...] From my room there leads off a terrace [...] from which one can view a small formal garden with fountain, after which there is an apparently limitless vista of scrubland, v. parched & dry-looking with small rather stunted trees here and there. The bird-life is fantastically colourful & noisy, the butterflies equally wonderful in colour (they look like pieces of painted rice-paper, c. twice the size of our Peacocks) & the flies are innumerable. Despite the presence high (v. high – it's a huge room) on the ceiling of my room of a tarantula last night, I would have slept very well were it not for the depredations of a single mosquito which would not go away. Should sleep well tonight, tho', & am feeling quite OK - about to take a couple of hours rest. All I hope is I'm running into form, because I want to play well to reward people for their marvellous generosity & openness. It's like California without the hang-ups. Tomorrow to Brisbane for a seminar & evening recital, foll. by mid-day recital, seminar, and return to Armidale the next day. [...]

61

John to Monica
9.10.80
(Hand-written)

Location unknown,
possibly Armidale

Probably my last letter [...] [Dalby] recital went pretty well – I played well, I feel, but the piano was really duff – [...] all the notes, but the piano is as wide as it is long! – Wendy Lorenz warned me about it. [...] Brisbane was marvellous. Again v. hectic – arrived motel 1pm, 2-hour lecture at 2, some practice, evening recital. Both events were highly successful - smallest audience I've had at recital for 20 years [...] But lovely piano, & I played really well! Next day at Uni, mid-day recital & afternoon lecture, both again went well [...] Ride back from Brisbane was at night, but even then I sensed that it was a spectacular ride, just going W. of Mount Flinders through a mountain pass, road lined with tropical rainforest. Sky clear, what a lot of stars there are up there – incredible sight!

3 Composition Seminars yesterday & today, + today mid-day on Mod. Brit. Pno. Music &, later, rehearsal of concertos. [...]

Wendy Lorenz was the pianist of the Australian Piano Trio, together with her husband, Andrew (violin) and Janis Laurs (cello). They became very good friends, and later premiered John's piano trio commissioned by Earle Page College, Desert III: Landscape. This visit, which also took in Sydney, and subsequent visits to Australia, had an enormous effect on John's composition, with both the Deserts and Rainforests series of works, and also the orchestral tone-poem, Fire at Durilgai.

62

From Richard Rodney Bennett
Undated, but some time in 1981
(Hand-written)

NY 10019

How nice of you to write. Glad you like the songs. I wrote them suddenly & because I wanted to, unlike what I'm writing now. [...] I'm thrilled about being No. 6 on your Top of the Pops. I do want to get back to writing piano music & think it's time for a large second sonata, since twenty-seven years (HELP) have gone by since the small first sonata, which was largely written in the gents' waiting-room at the R.A.M. because I was too shy to go into the cafeteria. I'm very fascinated with the recent music of Henri Dutilleux & wonder if you know the excellent piano sonata? [...] I'm at present struggling with trumpet, clar., vln., d.bass & piano, which must be the foulest combination in the world. One hour's isolation at a time is quite enough; then I leap out and watch TV or play records or buy books. In fact, writing this letter is a cunning way of avoiding thinking of a first bar. [...] I have Jane and Tony coming to stay soon & must practise being a Good Listener. [...] I <u>must</u> try to write some music [...]

Richard is writing from New York, where he has now settled. The songs mentioned were probably Vocalese, 1981, written for Jane Manning and John. No Second Piano Sonata appears ever to have been written. The reference to being No. 6 on John's Top of the Pops may possibly refer to John's frequent playing of Richard's piano works, especially during the Middle East tour. Jane was well-known for being talkative.

63

From Nicholas Maw
23 September '81
(Hand-written)

40, Oak Village,
London NW5.

[…] Firstly the question of the choice of artists for The Voice of Love centred entirely on the singer. The Arts Council were very keen to get hold of Sarah Walker (for obvious reasons) and I certainly was not going to quarrel with them about that. […] Nobody is more aware than I am how much you have done on behalf of The Voice of Love, and Personae as well. I am all the more indebted to you for two reasons: not being a performer myself I am obliged to rely on the goodwill and enthusiasm of performers such as yourself to launch my works, and so often you have been the <u>only</u> pianist who has performed both these works. […]

The question of Kent Opera is rather different […] All I know is that about ten years ago they asked me to think about writing something for them […] I have been in touch with them on and off ever since […] I finally decided (after they had made me a more serious offer) […] that if I were going to write another opera, they were the only company at present who I really wanted to write for. So I agreed […] I don't know whether the BBC had anything to do with all this, but I certainly share your unspoken feeling that the BBC commissioning policy is very odd at best and appallingly biased at worst. Perhaps I should point out in this context that I have only ever had one straight BBC commission (Scenes and Arias in <u>1962</u>, fee £100), and that it was not until eighteen years later that I had another, and that was only because the Edinburgh Festival twisted their arm […]

While I don't possess John's original letter to Nicholas (Nick, as he would generally have been known to John) it seems that he is sore with him on two different points. John had performed The Voice of Love many times with Meriel Dickinson, and indeed his Concertante Variations on a Theme of Nicholas Maw is based on this work. He clearly felt that any recording of the piece should have been offered to Meriel and himself, though this is not to suggest that he had anything other than the greatest admiration for Sarah Walker. John is obviously also annoyed that a projected opera for Kent Opera, based on Hardy's Under The Greenwood Tree, has been suddenly dropped, possibly in favour of an opera by Nick, who ends with a melancholy complaint of his own. A holiday was curtailed in order to attend the first European performance of Scenes and Arias. On arrival in Brussels, they found it had been cancelled. The association between John and Nick was of too long-standing to be affected by a tiff. Gripes about BBC commissions were, and probably still are, commonplace among composers. In the end, I believe neither John's opera, nor the one projected by Maw, ever happened. The letter from Nicholas covers six pages, but the above is the essence of it.

To Ian and Elizabeth Hird
11.10.81
(Typed)

Southall

Many thanks for your letter of August 5th - dear me, how time does go! I hope the exhibit went well, and you're busy and gainfully employed, as they say. I envy you your St. Ives holiday, though we did manage a few days in the Lake District a short while ago (after the weather had turned nasty, naturally) – nearly got blown off the side of Great Gable, which cleared away a few cobwebs [...]

I'm not quite sure when we were last in touch – I suspect it was when you rang, and I'd already been to Hong Kong by then. In May I went to the country to write a piece and got a mild attack of pneumonia, but I seem to be OK now and am getting ready for the onslaught of the season. November sees me off to the States for a spell of c. 3 weeks – New York twice, Pittsburgh (where Previn's doing the Hartmann Variations, as well as in NY), San Diego, Redlands (California), and possibly Boston and one or two other Eastern places [...] Next June I'm off to Australia again, to which I am especially looking forward – I was bowled over by the place the first time (a year ago, now) and absolutely loved it. The landscape really is fascinating [...] it has a special mystery and size to it.

Lots of concerts this season, which makes composition rather tricky – it looks as if I'll spend Christmas writing as usual. I'm supposed to be doing a piano trio for an Australian group as well as the quartet for the Delme and [a] Concerto for Orchestra for the London Philharmonic – those are the main things. It's all up to schedule for the moment but only by dint of being in grave danger of falling behind schedule at any moment (ie there's no urgency yet about [any] of these pieces, but they will all start to become urgent about the same time).

Have spent the last three days catching up on "office work" – bills, letters, trying to work out programmes for the 82/83 season, and so on. I've decided to resurrect a few items of previous repertoire after a long gap – the Brahms Handel Variations and Fugue (I quite agree with your liking for variations), some Mozart pieces, and some French repertoire (Satie and Ravel) as well as the usual things. I've also decided to make each of the four programmes I'll be offering to give a special prominence to one composer, with three works or groups of short pieces in the concert: Schumann, Haydn, Mozart and Schubert (a set of variations and one sonata in his case) are the composers and I think I've worked out some nice programmes. I fully expect all sorts of alterations to be suggested as I go along, but it's a start anyway. It's great fun working out programmes, but incredibly frustrating (all the wonderful stuff that can't be programmed). But this time I'll have to stick pretty rigidly to this repertoire, even if the programmes are occasionally reshuffled if people want them to be – I can't go on playing 100 different pieces in a season!

It's my ambition this month to do some work on all my repertoire for the season as well as being ready for the concerts in November – that should allow me time to compose during the leaner spells and prepare properly when the time comes. One of the problems of doing a lot of concerts is that, with the travelling, one has less time to prepare the repertoire for each concert as one goes along, so more work has to be done by way of preparation, which in turn means that 3 or 4 programmes are the most one can [carry?] and even then little of the repertoire can be new additions. It's fascinating working it all out though.

And I must get back to it […] Incidentally, the Kelso Study (the Mary Queen of Scots Paraphrase) will I hope be coming into print next year, and I'm also hoping that I'll record it before too long. […]

John is obviously hitting the typewriter running, in this letter – hence the odd missing word. He is also clearly still thinking out loud about his programmes. Ian and Elizabeth - quite apart from being musical – were both potters. Ian made pottery for use – plates, platters, soup- bowls, and such-like, in the russet, green, grey and light blue colours of the Scottish border country; Elizabeth made splendid large-scale pottery models of vernacular Scottish houses. All three of the compositions were completed on time: the piano trio was the previously-mentioned Desert III: Landscape, for the Australian Piano Trio, while the Concerto for Orchestra was premiered at the Royal Festival Hall by Solti, who later took it to the Chicago Symphony Orchestra.

From Robert Simpson
19.X.81
(Hand-written)

Chearsley

Delighted to get your letter! I'd like to write you a long one, but I've got to rush to get to the post with a lot of other letters. I must say I'm fed up with the way the whole Prom thing has been misrepresented by all and sundry, sometimes deliberately by people who want to please the BBC. The Listener correspondence has got totally side-tracked by aggrieved composers, etc., &

I wish someone would bring it back to the <u>principle</u>, which is the only thing that matters. I'm tired of writing letters of that kind, and if I do it too often, I'll appear to be out on a limb. If only the <u>profession</u> would come out into the open! Are they <u>all</u> scared? You and Patric weren't. If you jump in now, your role in the book will make it seem like collusion – but <u>please</u> try to get somebody to do it if you can. However, it all had to be said, and I've never been naïve enough to suppose it would bear fruit.

The book referred to is The Proms and Natural Justice, published Toccata Press 1981. John did not receive an orchestral Prom commission until 2014, the year before his death. I think that 'Patric' was Patric Standford. I have no letters to show what if any was the response by John to Bob Simpson's letter.

66

From John to Monica
14 Nov. 1981
(Postcard)

Pittsburgh went splendidly – the whole thing was a very big deal & seems to have gone well. Excellent review for Liszt Fantasy in N.Y. Spectacular performance by Previn – best I've heard (slightly steadier than most, & thus more cumulative). Weather splendid – am waiting at L.A. for connection to San Diego.

This was part of a wide-ranging trip in the USA, as explained in a previous letter to me, dated 10/11/81, which however was largely about travel arrangement (and problems), hotels, practising arrangements and so forth. Apart from Pittsburgh and New York, John was in Philadelphia, Redlands, and San Diego. The main focus of the trip, however, was performances of John's Hartmann Variations under Previn, in Pittsburgh and New York, part of a British Music Festival. The Liszt Fantasy is an early piano work of John's, which was played by another pianist on this occasion.

From Denis Forman
25 January 1982
(Typed)

Novello & Company Ltd.,
1-3, Upper James Street,
London W1R 4BP.

The book about John Field is called 'The Life and Music of John Field' by Patrick Piggott [...] It is a very interesting account of his life, and incidentally I own a Clementi square piano which from its serial number and date make it virtually certain that John Field tested it in person and may, I'd like to think, have used it for demonstration.

Sir Denis Forman was the CEO of Granada Television, then second only (if that) to the BBC in Britain. He was responsible for many fine programmes, including the series, The Jewel in the Crown. However, his connection with John was via Novellos, which Granada had purchased, probably because of Sir Denis's interest in music. He wrote a book on Mozart Piano Concertos, and was responsible for the TV programme about John writing his orchestral work, The Chagall Windows.

From John Casken
27 January 1982
(Hand-written)

Hatfield College,
Durham DH1 3RQ.

A few, very brief words to thank you once again for your marvellous playing of my Concerto. It was a great privilege to write it for you and to be able to work on it with you over the past few days. I learnt a lot and was greatly encouraged in spite of the beefy orchestration. I <u>am</u> sorry I failed to give you more solo writing [...]

In John Casken's score it was requested that the piano be placed in the middle of the orchestra. This did not work out well, balance-wise, and especially with John's comparatively light touch. John Casken withdrew the work for revision, and I believe that it has not been re-issued.

From Barney Childs
9 February 1982
(Typed)

University of Redlands,
School of Music.

Or maybe it's the 8th, a drizzly Monday in Redlands, that town which, to paraphrase the late Paul Goodman, brings out the second-best in everyone.

I'm just back from two days at your favourite West Coast university, UCLA, doing a session with their improvisation ensemble (listening <u>can</u> replace rushing blindly on, but I don't think I came close to convincing them of that) and one with their rookie composers ("Mr Childs, what are you trying to do in this piece?"). UCLA is just about to move into a vast & opulent new music building, the which I was given an extensive tour of. [...] I enclose some pretty stamps; surely you know someone whose nephew or grandchild collects them.

Picked up a catalogue from an East Coast outfit that sells by mail order records which firms have cut out and are remaindering. Not too happy to discover that the disc with my trio on't is on the list, but this is remedied somewhat by a couple of other entries: "Pope John Paul II Sings (ALL selections in Polish)", and "Jesus Christ Superstar, original German cast (in German)". Oh well, who wants to hear three-oboe pieces anyway?

Yes, I am familiar with John Casken's work – we've done Visu I here twice - and I share your appreciation of it. Your concertising seems as extensive as ever. My conscience upbraids me for sitting drunken in front of the TV of evenings when I should be Composing Great Masterworks. Did manage to run off a 2-clarinet piece for two of our local graduate students. So far the title has not suggested itself, but I'm inclining towards <u>Real Music</u>, as in "Why don't you ever write any real music?". There is thought being given towards a request by telephone a couple of weeks ago: "Of course they can't pay anything, but there are several performances scheduled." It's the "of course" that gets to me. I seem to attract freak instrumental combinations (probably my own fault based on certain past ensemble choices): this one's 3 violas and 3 trombones.

Of course I'll forward programmes etc. from the <u>Images</u> performance of the CBDNA regional. Glad you liked what you heard of the premiere. [...] My daughter writes from Thailand, where The Church has sent her to teach English to Cambodian refugees for six months [...] Her descriptions of what furnishes forth the table at important native banquets could have been omitted from her letter with advantage. I agree with your approbation of Tinker Tailor [...] I'm watching Brideshead Revisited instalments [...] Final judgement still to be made.

I have been sent a copy of a new book to review for a new magazine. The book is interviews with 24 American composers. The selection is heavily weighted in favour of New York Biggies, and the questions seem to have been planned to elicit extensive meandering and pretentious responses. It's a dandy book for your reg'lar down-home B-flat library researcher, but it's nowhere as a bedside companion. I'd almost rather hear Phil Glass's music than […] but wait a minute….

The British export bureau is getting sloppy, letting out material which is best kept at home. I refer to a facsimile page in the new Perspectives of Brian Ferney-hough's La Terre est un Homme (can't the man use his native tongue?); 55 staves, at least one measure with something happening on all of them, and the something appears (my eyesight ain't wot it useter be) to be not just different for each instrument, but incredibly complicated. The sound probably buggers [*sic*] description. On second thoughts: the magazine's editor didn't have to include it. Black mark for our side.

[*Phil*] Rehfeldt and I have been playing Clarinet and Friend concerts recently, mostly noon-hour concerts at local seats of learning. We are, however, going to perform not only at the American Society of University Composers (I real-ise that the acronym of this is far from ideal, but it beats the hell out of the American Symphony Orchestra League) in Seattle (big national conference) in April and the National Clarinet Clinic in Denver in August, but also at Northern Arizona University, this last vital because a) we will be getting an enormous sum, probably almost what we're worth and b) of all the commis-sions we have given, the one I play…..least well. (OK, OK, the one I can barely play at all) was written by the man who has arranged to bring us to Northern Arizona University.

Next day: May be a considerable improvement. Wotcha got for viola? Local violista is looking for some pieces, just looking, but should you have a piece I can have her write to Novello. I have stopped telling violists about my solo sonata, finished in 1956 and not yet premiered. Eleven (or maybe 12?) good strong players have asked excitedly for the work over the intervening years; there must be something Medusan in the thing because it strikes them instantly into endless silence. […] The most recent was a lady at Memphis State who all but promised the premiere…..for all I've heard about it since she might as well be one with Ninevah and Tyre.

[*David*] Maslanka is doing damn well these days; commissions of substance, a couple performances of his concerto for piano and winds-and-percussion (OK, band) (a dazzlingly impressive piece which is in the refreshing tradition of forgetting completely about the lickey Bandness of so much of the literature – by the way (digression) I think this is just the reason your band piece works so well […] that you have no native concert band tradition cluttering your sense of

From Monica to Ian and Elizabeth Hird
Feb. 22nd 1983
(Typed)

Southall

It seems a very long time since we were up staying with you, that very delightful (if rather cold!) Easter we spent at your house [...] As I remember, the previous time I was your way I had the mother and father of a cold. That, I think, was when John first performed the enclosed work. Poor soul – travelling around Scotland with me, either sneezing or coughing, or unable to speak or swallow – and him with lots of concerts to play, and me too weak and ill to be able to drive back to London alone.

You must excuse our being so much out of touch with you since then. Last year was a real......well, let's say it was very busy. John did certain things like writing a Concerto for Orchestra (recently premiered) in two weeks, going on a 5-week tour of Australia playing two concertos and lots of assorted recitals, including a set of 6 different recitals on a classical theme, without having been able to practise the said recitals first, because he was too busy getting the Concerto finished. That sort of thing. The pressure kept up all year, and although there certainly were some highlights......by November John was just about buggered – please excuse the language, but it's the only suitable word. I was certainly worried about him, especially as he had two recitals at the Belfast Festival, which he fulfilled against my wish, but he was ill both before and after Christmas. Only minor illnesses – flu, that sort of thing - but obviously very tired and run-down. I think he/we are just about on our feet again. [...]

I often look at your evocative pottery, which I love just as much now as when I first bought it. [...] Meanwhile I hope you are both keeping very well and happy. [...] And please accept this inscribed copy of the 'Mary, Queen of Scots' Paraphrase, with our love.

That John tackled his six different recitals on a Classical theme without prior practice is a bit of an exaggeration. He would have been familiar with most of the works, which only required a degree of refurbishment. He had, I think, also played the Haydn D major Concerto before.

From John to Monica
10.3.83
(Postcard)

Barcelona

This is a lovely place for a holiday – fascinating city, lively atmosphere, splendid buildings. Thought you'd like a sample of the <u>real</u> Gaudì. Writing this awaiting rehearsal.

The postcard is of a corner of Güell Park, with Gaudì steps. The rehearsal would be of the Concerto for Orchestra, with the London Philharmonic Orchestra and Solti.

From Steve Martland
25/3/83
(Hand-written)

Oranje Plein 64,
2515 Den Haag,
Netherlands.

I'm just writing to say that I'm coming to London on Monday 4th April to hear a performance of my 'duo' for trumpet + piano in the Purcell Room on Wed. 6th. Also to let you know that my piano piece has won the International Stockhausen piano composition competition in Italy. I got the news the other day and ignored the letter because it was in Italian. It was only later that I spotted my name! As you can imagine I'm amazed by it all – it's taken me by surprise. I have to go to Bergamo on June 7th to get the prize and hear a performance. Actually it's come at a good time because I am broke and every penny is counting for a lot just now. […]

82

From Barney Childs
17 May 83
(Typed)

Redlands,
California.

By the time this arrives […] you may well have returned from Albany etc. I take typewriter in hand, so to speak, to thank you for coming out & being about. […] At least you got rid of the cold; I am just now getting rid of it. Thank a bunch!

I've been reading the Graham Greene books you so kindly provided, and they are curious, not quite what one might expect from an autobiography of such a one: his early childhood is almost the textbook sort of thing one (or anyway, I) expect(s) well-brought-up English children of that time to have had, with all the rich detailing one has come to hope for, but I can't believe that his conversion to and persistence in Catholicism was as much of less personal consequence than the lack of space devoted to it suggests. I have trouble with books of this nature keeping at bay any tendency to slip into (especially if the writer has slipp'd into) a kind of animistic view of the past, where that very richness of detail is held up as the reason one is as one is: because of this, therefore that. I think he's pretty good about avoiding the perils of 'Looking back at it now, I…..' and 'I scarcely could have suspected at the time that…..'. I am a bit put off by what seems a sort of continuo of reference to his own writings, especially early flops and unpublished efforts that the reader can hardly have knowledge of. But I suppose any kind of 'looking back' book runs all of these risks: autobiographies by non-famous people in their thirties, for example, wouldn't – don't – hold much interest. And that's a point I want to hold up in connection with the look back/causality business: how do 'follies and sentimentalities and exaggerations of the distant time' get to <u>be</u> that? Isn't it merely some judgement or evaluation that makes so activities and thinkings which at their time were the best one could come up with? Are one's earlier compositions quaint and archaic and less of value on some ex-post-facto esthetic meter stick than the ones one is doing now? If I/you wanted to write them differently at that time we would have done so. All esthetic choices are the best choices. Even if one is trying purposely to write a bad piece, say an assortment of present or past clichés, he picks out the best bad bits he can to include.

I spent a few moments wondering what my autobiography would be like, and it wouldn't be that interesting: but hold! If one were a good enough writer, wouldn't the details of any childhood and youth, say, be equally well-presented and of equal interest? (I'm not discussing the grown-up part, because Greene's life was unique – because there's nothing like it, of course. […]

As examination papers say, 'Discuss'. I can think of several autobiographies of childhood written by 'non-famous' writers, and indeed unpractised writers, which hold up Barney's theory, among them Lark Rise to Candleford (Flora Thompson) and the Mancunian trilogy by Margaret Penn (beginning Manchester 14 Miles). Period Piece, by Gwen Raverat doesn't quite fall into the same category, because of the people she knew.

83

To Ian and Elizabeth Hird from Monica
July 26th 1983
(Typed)

Southall

Please excuse (usual) late, and hasty reply to your letter. A great many things have happened to us since we met in Kelso in April – 1) John was in the US for 5 weeks and on return (the very same day) injured his hand so badly that he is only today playing the piano for the first time. I might add that despite all our fears and tremblngs at the beginning, he seems to me to be playing just as easily today as if there had been no 9-week break in between. Indeed it is his elbow (damaged in Spain in Feb.) which is causing him more actual discomfort. (And no, he isn't particularly accident-prone – it's just been one of those years.)

2) (numbered paragraphs, you see) His father, who has been ailing and in hospital for much of the last year, died about a month ago, and John, being the only child, had much to do to get everything organised, and spent quite a lot of time with his mother in Liverpool (not to mention quite a lot of time on trains between here and there).

3) His year of office as president of the ISM is taking up a lot of time at present. He seems to be in London for meetings about two days a week. […]

4) After a lot of persuasion, John has agreed to take on the job of Director of the London College of Music, which he takes up in September. We sincerely hope that this is not going to take up too much time – indeed John only under-took it after promises that he would not be expected to drop his true career as composer and pianist. They seem to have a very good administrator there, who is quite happy to hold all the reins while John decides on the direction to be taken. John has a lot of plans for the place, including developing it as a centre for Composition Studies, with which the Powers seem to be very happy. It's quite a little College – the smallest of the London Big Five, but it has a lot of things going for it, including the fact that it owns its own (Central London) premises, and that it is privately run and financed, and consequently is not particularly affected by the present Government education cuts. […]

No – haven't read the novel you speak of (CAL). Have just re-read 'Old Mortal-ity', which is pretty good, I think, tho' a bit long-winded in parts. The revolutionary bits (Cameronians) and the local life is excellently well done. Only the upper-crust lovers are a bit unbearable.

And that is ALL!

This is not the place to comment at length on John's time at the London College of Music. Unfortunately the 'good administrator' died in office, after about two years, leaving John with all the reins in his hands.

84

From Barney Childs
Kalends of August 83
(Typed)

Redlands,
California.

[…] Running onto the phrase used by the author of the big new Elliott Carter book, High Modernism (the phrase, not the book's title) has given me furiously for to think: why does everyone have to be so damn serious in what one writes? Pomposity, avaunt! That's one of the reasons I like the fiddle concerto you played, no futzing about, one can launch oneself as a listener into a marvellous sea of sound and effect and colour and opulence and thus ENJOY and savor: if music isn't any fun at all why the hell do we bother with all the ridiculous work? I'm not precluding the serious, no way, it's just that I'm goldurn tahred of being repeatedly slipped down that current between the Scylla of novelty-mongering and the Charybdis of Significant Serious Musick.[…]

Much of this letter is light-hearted: this is the end part only. The fiddle concerto must have been John's Second Violin Concerto. I'm somewhat surprised that Barney liked this big-boned, opulent work – but then, like John, he was very broadminded in his approach to music.

85

From Richard Rodney Bennett
Dated only Sept. 7, but written in 1983
(Hand-written)

NY 10019 ?

[…] I was very sad to hear of your father dying […] In fact my own mother died at the end of the week I saw you at Dartington. I rushed up there on the Saturday & she died quietly on the Sunday. Then there was all the gruelling business of lawyers, undertakers etc […] to be dealt with.

So now I'm back, in punishing heat, trying to write what Americans strangely call a Woodwind Quintet, never my favourite combination […] I think a live performance of the Schönberg is my idea of living death […] You both played my sonata absolutely marvellously, whether or not you could read the music (a likely story). […]

Excerpts from a somewhat subdued letter from Richard in New York, sympathising with John on the death of his father. A letter to him from John had only just been picked up. The sonata was presumably the Violin Sonata, with Erich Gruenberg.

86

From Richard Rodney Bennett
Dated only Oct. 8th , but written in 1983
(Hand-written)

101 W 81st # 204,
New York, NY 10024.

Your letter of Sept. 13 didn't arrive the day after I left for London as you feared; it arrived today, almost a week after I returned, because you <u>hadn't stamped</u> it properly, so it came over very slowly, like early immigrants. […]

I had (forgive me for saying so) a <u>smashing</u> piece done at Windsor while I was over recently. It's called 'Memento' – flute & 12 strings & will be done at St. J. Smith Square in Nov. some time & maybe you could make a trip up West to hear it! I'm specially fascinated because it's <u>not serial</u>!! I may just possibly have made it out, along with G. Rochberg, D. Bedford, Penderecki & C. Wuorinen (*sic*). And of course yourself. Am still grinding away at my wind quintet but LIKING it, except that it's rather like writing Götterdämerung (only as regards the effort involved, not in musical style) – thanks to my new-found freedom, which feels rather like tight-rope walking sans net.

After saying (rather publicly) recently that I was doing No More Films, I have now been offered a tv 'mini-series' – 7 hours, not what I wd normally call mini – called The Last Days of Pompeii. The largest set ever built, Laurence Olivier, 2 hours music & an untold amount of money (I hope). I know a perfectly splendid girl ondes Martenot player in London whom I will use & and also thought I might put in 2 <u>large</u> piano parts, one for S. Bradshaw. Just out of curiosity would you be appalled at the idea of doing the other? Don't know if you do that class of work. Let me know sometime. I'm fairly thrilled (mostly about the money), but nothing is yet fixed, so not a word to a soul (except Mrs. McC) or

Dame Fortune will punish me & Andrew Lloyd Webber will get the gig. Sorry to upset you about the Schxxxxrg Wind Quintet. […]

PPS Susan Bradshaw said recently that I am TOTALLY uncritical of my music – tho' not, presumably, while writing it. Am terribly afraid she is right.

WORRIED BROWN EYES.

Dame Fortune did punish Richard, as you will see from a following letter, but it was not through John's indiscretion. I am dating this letter 1983, because John has ticked it as replied to on 16/11/83. It appears that Richard has moved to a new apartment during this period.

From Marjorie Coombs
27/10/83
(Hand-written)

49 Holmesdale Road,
Dronfield,
Sheffield.

Your letter was very interesting and I became quite nostalgic remembering you as a tiny boy sitting in Rostherne garden absorbing Grade V Theory! and playing Walter Carroll's Farm Tunes! […]

I can't with certainty pin down the writer of this letter, but I believe she must have been Marjorie Madge, John's very first piano teacher. I believe she was still a young woman at this time. Nostalgia all round, as I also played Walter Carroll's piano music for beginners – but not attempting to absorb Grade V Theory at the same time.

From Richard Rodney Bennett
Dated only Nov. 25th, but almost certainly 1983

No address

Holst <u>is</u> a better composer. Much. That is my last word on the subject. Except that if you want living proof, try playing VW's Intro & Fugue for 2 pnos, as Comrade B & I did not long ago (we were mistakenly asked to record it) &

nearly fell dead with boredom. And <u>that</u> is my last word on the subject. I think I prefer E.J. Moeran. When I was 13 I thought the Concerto Accademico (spelling?) was simply splendid, & tried to write it. And you should see my 1st string quartet, written at the age of 14. But I learned my error & the 2nd quartet is strictly Schoenberg 4-tet no. 3 (aged 17). I worked out with the aid of my calculator & the metronome speed, that the Intro & Fugue lasts 17 mins; it consists entirely of very thick & bad counterpoint all in C minor at the same tempo. Like having to eat 3 tons of old, <u>old</u> bread pudding. And that is my last word etc.

I do not have time to waste on idle chat. I am in the middle of a compositional jag hitherto unpara [*crossed out*].....unparral.....unequalled. I finished the famous wind quintet & immediately started quite a nice piece for chorus (15 mins) based on bits from The Tempest & the day after I finished it thought of a good idea for a piece for Tessa Cahill & the Sinfonietta. [...] The usual Mad Lady bit. That was going OK when I suddenly thought of doing a big piece for guitar which <u>nobody had asked for</u>, so I started that & wrote a frantic 1st movt. And I still have a piece for tenor and orch. unfinished. It's quite fun in a terrifying way, but will doubtless end in tears & grief and frightfull – sorry – ful reviews ("shows his usual facility, but has no heart, soul or character of any kind"). [...]

I could be writing Mad Lady music instead of drivelling on like this. If we keep it up we can publish a slim volume of letters.

You are lucky to be <u>able</u> to play Miroirs; I would give anything to play that piece, also the Bartok studies & Debussy Etudes (2 vols.). [...] The Last Days of Pompeii went to someone I've never heard of but I do have a movie called The Ebony Tower (John Fowles, with L. Olivier – ugh), & if you are free (late Jan [...]) will write you a dazzling keyboard part, ditto Susan & a dear friend of mine who is a crack girl ondes Martenot player. [...] Back to the Mad Lady music.

PS That is my last word.

Richard back to high spirits again - sheets of paper in his incredible enormous hand-writing, full of underlinings. John and he had been arguing the respective merits of Holst and Vaughan Williams. John was an ardent VW fan. Comrade B is Susan Bradshaw, with whom Richard had an occasional piano duet partnership. The Ebony Tower score was for Granada TV, and John did undertake a piano part in it, with Susan Bradshaw, and the ondes Martenot player Cynthia Millar. I have dated the letter 1983 because of the guitar work, written in 1983.

From Barney Childs
22 February 1984
(Typed)

Redlands,
California.

[…] Ample time before leaving for school this morning to listen to (senza hang-over; I must be getting immune) the fiddle concerto on the cassette; aside from occasional sounds of an audience member suffering obviously what is periodic and serious seizure….What a luxurious….and I mean that with more than a hint of Elizabethan meaning!....piece!....I still think my favourite movement is #2, a surprise every few bars, delight upon delight. How the hell does one learn to orchestrate? I can beat my head against the wall and the result is merely a bunch of separate instruments playing, not that marvellously malleable and ductile SOUND, which before you've fully asked HOW IS THAT BEING DONE? has changed and metamorphosed….against this usage, of course, solos become even more characteristic of those timbres and expressivities for which they have been selected. […]

I'm not sure of the Elizabethan meaning of 'luxurious' but suspect it carries more than a hint of carnality. Approbation indeed from Barney! It always surprised me how well John got on with such disparate characters as Richard and Barney, but I think he was very sensitive to individuality, and of course he respected both of them for their intelligence and abilities.

From Richard Rodney Bennett
Dated only April 10th, but written in the Spring of 1984
(Hand-written)

NY 10024?

[…] If this letter sounds mildly crazed it is because I have just finished a 10 minute FUNpiece for amateur orchestras for the National Federation of some-thing or other. I wish to put it on record that I am accepting <u>no more</u> commissions for jubilees, anniversaries, people's birthdays, children, amateurs, festive occasions etc. In future I shall only write for funerals, memorial services. <u>This</u> number ends with a relentlessly merry 3 minute section in 6/8 (suggestive of Ruth Gipps & Imogen Holst getting violently drunk together) which practically killed me & I felt as tho' it lasted 3 weeks instead of 3 mins. […]

This would have been the Sinfonietta, written for the National Federation of Music Societies 50th Anniversary in 1984. Richard also mentions in a PS having just written a carol for Ted Heath 'the politician, not the band-leader'.

91

From Richard Rodney Bennett
Dated only Thursday, but almost certainly 1984
(Hand-written, in red ink)

NY 10024?

Please excuse this paper [...] I have quite run out of my usual cheap typing paper, flowered notelets with diamante treble clefs etc. [...] It was a pleasure to have you playing on the session. I have a pretentious French thriller to do in the summer, recording in London, & I will write you a major Hammond organ part. I think Susan was v. shocked by the ondes Martenot (too sensuous) but I still think it was lovely.

Talking of sensuous, I'm starting a piece for Tessa Cahill (gorgeous voice) & the London Sinfonietta, settings of violently passionate sonnets by Louise Labé (1522-66, she died exhausted) who, as I was thrilled to discover, had such a reputation as a "grande amoureuse" that 400 years after her death the authorities of Lyons decided against naming a girls' school after her…..It's again one of those agony non-serial pieces & I'm not sure that I have the faintest idea what I am doing, except that it should sound orgiastic, which is what I always <u>meant</u> my music to sound like, but the series got in the way. I said before that writing non-serial music (except for the movies & for kiddies) was like tight-rope walking; now I think it's like skating on <u>very</u> thin ice. I find myself deep in a welter of phoney <u>counterpoint</u> (!!) which I never could write at all, since Dr. William Cole (!) wouldn't teach it to me.

We needn't discuss VW at all; I have Spoken My Mind.

I will certainly get in touch in late Feb., when I'm doing a very odd concert at the Barbican. [...] I have insanely said I will play the Falla hpschd concerto (& the Lambert) at Edinburgh, & cannot imagine why, since I don't even like it. So you may get a sudden call & had better start practising. Should that be 'practicing' or is that doctors?

R. Bennett FRAM, ARAM, CBE, D.SC. (Aston). All styles, classical to modern.

92

From John Corigliano
May 16 1984
(Typed)

NY 10024

Here are the two tapes I promised you: Flute and Clarinet concerti, and the piano works. […] I enjoyed meeting you and am looking forward to our working together on the <u>Piano Concerto.</u> Please send a tape of the Solti-Chicago performance [*of John's Concerto for Orchestra*] if you can spare one – I would love to hear it (and congratulations on the great notices) […]

Solti liked John's Concerto for Orchestra so much (premiered by the LPO in London) that he took it to Chicago to give the US premiere with his 'other' orchestra, the Chicago Symphony Orchestra. John was to give the first UK performance of Corigliano's brilliant but demanding Piano Concerto, in a BBC studio broadcast.

93

From Dr. Alan Bush
(The use of his title was requested by his descendents)
June 2nd 1984
(Typed)

25 Christchurch Crescent,
Radlett,
Herts. WD7 8AQ.

As a member of the ISM I receive their MUSIC JOURNAL and read your interesting article on 'The Place of Music in Society'. It recalled to me vividly the first performance of Michael Tippett's 'A Child of our Time', which took place in 1941 and which I attended.

As I read through your very substantial article I experienced growing surprise and disappointment that it contained no mention of a single other British work except Vaughan Williams's Tallis Fantasia, when there are quite a number of works which are concerned with the problem of social conditions and man's struggle to improve them.

Several operas by Benjamin Britten and my own four operas have as their subjects problems which are directly concerned with the place of man in society and man's struggle for a better social organisation than we in Western Europe have as yet established. Britten's operas enjoyed many performances and my four have received to date in all twelve professional productions in ten different European opera houses with a total of sixty or more actual performances. All four have been broadcast by the BBC.

A great many musical works by leading European composers have dealt with the place of man in society, if not the place of music in society. I feel that this feature of musical creation should have been mentioned in your interesting article.

94

To Dr. Alan Bush
June 16ᵗʰ 1984
(Typed)

Southall

Many thanks for your letter of June 2nd and your interest in my Presidential Address [*to the ISM*]. I think I should stress that this was a <u>speech</u>, to last no more than 30 minutes, and not an article – this meant, of course, that the number of topics I could cover was limited, as was the detail into which I could go. As you rightly say, the place of man in society has been dealt with by a great many composers, including yourself. However, my address was specifically designed not as a philosophical treatise but as a discussion of some of the practical and organisational barriers that exist in society today to the wider propagation of classical music. Had I an hour in which to speak, I might well have been able to deal with the completely different range of topics suggested in your letter, and I shall be delighted to do so if ever the opportunity occurs.

John's speech had been given at the final dinner during the weekend Conference concluding his year as President of the Incorporated Society of Musicians.

95

From Ian Partridge
July 3ʳᵈ 1984
(Hand-written)

London SW20

Just a note saying that I so much enjoyed our Concert in Aldeburgh last month. A hectic programme, which seemed to go quite smoothly. […] As for the ISM, that was a lovely day for me. It was nice to see so many people we hadn't seen for so long. I hope perhaps you might be able to relax a bit during the summer after your heavy ISM year. I went to the Test Match last Saturday (a wonderful day in every way) – but when I got back Ann had placed a copy of Elgar's 'Apostles' in the hallway. Harlow Society had rung during the day & needed a St. John. I don't recommend a day in the sun before a heavy concert of that nature. Still, I survived!!! – Just!

Ian Partridge, Ifor James and John had performed a mixed recital programme at Aldeburgh. The last item was Britten's setting of Edith Sitwell's Still Falls the Rain, a serious work leaving a deep impression on the audience. John's setting of D'ye ken John Peel was not perhaps a good choice as an encore. Ian had been reluctant, and was proved right, but it was chosen because it involved all the performers. Ian was lucky that mobile phones had not been invented at this time, or he would not have enjoyed his wonderful day at the Test Match. It must have been a close-run thing for the Harlow Society, who had presumably 'lost' their original choice.

96

To the Marketing Director, Peugeot Talbot
July 7th 1984
(Typed)

Southall

(John is amused to receive a targeted marketing letter from Peugeot Talbot, utilising the new skills of a computer. Sadly the computer is not fully trained. John has decided to reply in the same mode.)

Mr Chris Ho Are

Marketing Director, Peugeot Talbot

Dear Mr Are,

It certainly <u>is</u> all happening at my local Peugeot Talbot dealer this Summer! Pride of place in your Summer Numbers Game Brochure is given to a very special name – mine. Strange thing is, the spelling of this Special Name is different almost every time!

This name could be mine – glancing at the right of your letter I can indeed see my own unique 'Name'. Mr Hoare, it is sometimes spelt differently <u>twice on the same page</u>! Have you ever wondered, Mr. Re, if Special Edition Prizes were offered to people whose names can be spelt in so many different ways? What's more, if your letters were addressed to both myself and a relative of the same 'Name', could those prizes be doubled? Perhaps, Mr Are, you would care to offer £250-worth of Special Edition Spelling Kits to the relative of the same name?

THERE ARE MORE WAYS OF SPELLING ANYONE'S NAME THAN YOU THINK!

If you take my name to your local Peugeot Talbot Dealer, Mr. Ho, you could win a free copy of the Oxford Dictionary of Celtic Surnames. For a limited period only, if accompanied by a friend or relative, you will also receive ABSOLUTELY FREE a special course in translating any version of my Special Name into 67 different languages. This will enable you or your company (or your friend, relative or dog) to mis-spell this Summer Numbers Game in more Marketing Target Areas than you realised before existed.

YOU GET MORE FOR MORE WITH THE SPECIAL EDITION OF MY NAME!

So don't wait until it's too late. Take this Exclusive Entry Letter to your Local Education Authority today, Mr. Oare!

John McCabe (Named Person)

PS. Almost forgot! My name is in an ongoing relevance situation, so unlike the Summertime Special it doesn't run out on August 11th 1984!

Having amused himself by writing this squib, I don't think that John bothered to send it.

97

To Monica
Nov 6/84
(Card)

[…] Sitting here in Washington airport waiting for the NY flight, feeling hot & sticky […] Hollins College is beautiful campus, old (real old – 1840s), set amidst rolling, tree-clad Virginia hills. It was a disappointing visit, tho', because I didn't feel I played well. […] Lunch with Nick [*Maw*] was enjoyable. He already gives a guided tour, in some detail, & had sorted out the good eating places. No liquor – election day! (This means, since I gave the Sternbachs my bottle of Laphroaig […] I shall be bereft of sustenance at all until tomorrow!) You will be interested to know he [*Nick*] decided not to continue with the opera for Kent Opera for various reasons (inc. Norman Platt!) & had to repay the BBC his fee! We walked from the middle of town up to the Capitol building & the Library of Congress, where we peeked in at the L. of C. recital hall where so many great chamber works have been premiered, & where I bought some cards. Incl. this one, which I must finish, as we are about to be called. […]

See back to Nicholas Maw's letter to John of 23 September '81 [No. 63] for reference to Kent Opera. Nick had moved from England by this time to live in Washington, where he stayed for the rest of his life. He was well-known among friends for his ability to find the best places to eat, wherever he happened to be.

From William Mathias
24/11/84
(Hand-written)

Anglesey.

Many thanks for your kind letter, with its <u>very</u> helpful Violin Sonata 2 corrections – just the things I might not have spotted [...] Second (but really most important) a thousand thanks for that <u>marvellous</u> premiere of the new piece at Swansea. I am also writing to Erich to say I can hardly imagine it better done – you made it sound as though it had been in your repertoire for years. [...]

His Second Violin Sonata, dedicated to John and Erich Gruenberg, had been premiered at the Swansea Festival, October 1984.

From John Ogdon
December 22nd 1984
(Hand-written)

No address

I hope all is well with you – I remember as well your wonderful writings on Scriabine, and I hope you are composing as fecundly as ever; I was also so interested in your advocacy of performing more American music here – a strong need, I feel – and featuring English music more strongly generally in English Orchestral Programmes and in Recitals. [...]

He goes on to say that the main purpose of his letter is to introduce the German pianist Klaus Zoll, a pupil of Backhaus, and to mention that Zoll and violinist Madeleine Mitchell have performed Rawsthorne's Violin Sonata.

1985–1989

100

From Richard Rodney Bennett
Early 1985
(Hand-written)

En route

I'm writing this to while (wile?) away a flight from LA to San Francisco – and also of course because I wanted to answer yours of Jan. 6th. So in case the plane gets bumpy, and to quote the punch-line of a very old and vulgar joke (lady writing a letter complaining of her husband's rapacious behaviour) Excuse the wobbly writing.

Well, now. I hope the brass band piece is finished and is lovely. I don't seem to be able to write at <u>all</u> just now, wh. is very boring, but doubtless the knack will return. […] It could be a festive year (I am 50!!). […] I'm coming to England this May and June (new piece, as yet unwritten on May 20th at the QEH, Tender is the Night – 6 hours! - for the BBC TV and various mini-concerts) so maybe we can make some serious plans then. […] Am on the West Coast to play in various elegant jazz rooms & also to do a TV movie based on Agatha Christie & starring Helen Hayes, John Mills, Dorothy Tutin & unfortunately Bette Davis who has had a stroke & looks horrifying. The movie is very bad & I always find A. Christie boring and also incomprehensible, but I think I can do some nice music, aided as always by Miss Millar on the ondes.

 A friend of mine, a very famous black cabaret singer, was having lunch in Boston, keenly observed by a lady at the next table. She finally got up and <u>left</u> the restaurant, slipping a folded note beneath his plate. It read: 'Are you who I think you are?' Have been worrying <u>a lot</u> about that story. […]

The TV movie was possibly Murder with Mirrors – Warner.

101

From Patrick Thomas
2 March 1985
(Hand-written)

14 Boronia Avenue,
Turramurra,
NSW 2074.

Last night the SSO & I gave your Concerto for Orchestra its Australian premiere and the performance came off very well. <u>What a top piece</u>! Congratulations – you've done it AGAIN. The SSO members revelled in it and enjoyed the piece tremendously – even the hard-bitten pros! […]

Patrick Thomas was Conductor-in-Residence at the Sydney Symphony Orchestra, and at various other times, of other ABC orchestras. He had become a close, and indeed life-long friend of John's.

102

From Barney Childs
20 March 1985
(Typed)

Redlands,
California

[…] I'm off next Wednesday to give my "keynote" speech at the (deep breath) Twentieth National Conference of the American Society of University Composers […] While I dislike speakers who "view with alarm", a few choice sections are being prepared to pillory various noxious offenses. I may have mentioned that last year's speaker, Frank Zappa, got $5000 or so for his opening talk (in which we were told that academic composers were shits, in the precise words) and presence at the Conference (including performance of three of his orchestral pieces – these immediately previously having been recorded by Boulez at IRCAM, should your curiosity get the better of you […]); I find that I am getting $300 for speech and presence, and that suggests in turn some conclusions one had been on occasion previously led to. I am including the adjective "flatulent", however, which I think should raise the ante to at least $325. […]

Having closely studied the above passage, I suspect that Barney's ire slightly got the better of his prose style. I am reminded, as a sort of side-glance, of the time when the Times music critic William Mann applauded the Beatles as the best song-writers since Schubert.

From Richard Rodney Bennett
Marked only Sunday, probably early April 1985
(Hand-written)

No address

Dear Sir, I am writing to you because I am worried. We used to have quite a nice 'correspondance' (I have a passion for inverted commas wrongly used) & exchange quite a nice lot of amusing letters. However, I have noticed lately there has been 'silence' from your end (and from my end too). Am hoping I have not given offense in some way. Well Mr. McCabe I know how busy you are so will get to the 'point'. […]

I have no news apart from the fact that I was in Calif. for a month, hated San Francisco, loved L.A. for some strange reason, did a bad TV movie for a lot of money, came back & got the worst flu ever known (I think it was 'God' punishing me very swiftly) & thought quietly about dying. However after THREE WEEKS of feeling deathly I got into a huge writing jag & wrote 2 quite good pieces in the next three weeks! Just as well 'cos I hadn't written anything but wicked TV music since last September. One piece is for eleven solo strings (QEH May 20) in memory of W. Walton & as I told 'S. Bradshaw' will either sound very beautiful or just plain soppy. The other number is for horn & piano & is called (are you ready?) 'Romances'! (I think it was the flu, Spring etc.) It is for a recital here next Feb. by B.Tuckwell (who has also had appalling flu & said on the phone, had I had the kind where you go BLIND? Help) & yours truly at which I want to do one of the Goddess Trilogy. I am ever anxious to help a friend. Which reminds me I must talk to Ms. Snapp about our 2-piano venture. […] I have a perfectly good idea, title, etc, for a piece for us, tho' by now I should really know that ideas & titles have absolutely nothing to do with writing music. I am trying to write a piece for 'symphonic wind ensemble' (inv. commas perfectly justified here as it includes euphonium & 4 saxes) & have a perfectly good idea, title, etc. & cannot write a note. I thought it would be a good idea to listen to records of modren [*sic*] band music but got v. depressed…..I think Schönberg is repellent and as for the Hindemith Symphony. He uses a texture that sounds like an accordion going full blast in about 5 octaves all at once which is the single most horrid thing I've ever heard, tho' I missed Andrew Lloyd Webber's Requiem recently. […] I don't know why I'm rambling on like this. I could be watching TV.

I'll be over around May 7 & will be in London till about July 20; more wicked TV music & concerts & a newish piece (Guitar sonata, Bream) at Cheltenham. […] By the way did you know George [*Rizza*] was furiously bidding for A.L.W.'s

Requiem (can't spell that word. Requiem) & looked very sneaky when I yelled and screamed, & said it would be a huge money-maker. […]

I don't believe the 2-piano venture ever did materialise. John I think was in Australia at the time of this forlorn letter from Richard, and I was shortly to join him there. John was a big Hindemith fan, at least for his finest pieces, such as Ludus Tonalis and Mathis der Maler. I don't know what he thought about the Symphony Richard listened to. George Rizza was head of Novellos at that time.

104

From William Alwyn
May 7ᵗʰ 1985
(Hand-written)

Blythburgh

Thank you for your most kind letter of April 23rd. I'm delighted to know that you plan to give two performances of my Concerto for Flute and Eight Wind Instruments in honour of my eightieth birthday this year. Nothing could please me more. Mary and I would love to have been able to attend one of the performances, but since my stroke & meningitis four years ago I have become more or less immobile […]

The performances would have been by students at the London College of Music. In 2005 John made an arrangement of this work for flute and orchestra.

105

From John to Monica
May 10/85
(Hand-written)

Lennons Brisbane Hotel,
66 Queen Street, Brisbane,
Queensland 4000.

[…] I don't feel that I've settled down, for once – jet-lag was no problem, but believe it or not my new long-distance glasses are no longer quite right. It's better than the old ones, but I've got that slight second image again. […] The Brisbane Cultural Centre is quite splendid – nice to look at, good acoustics in the concert hall […] modern architecture at its best. […] The schedule is pretty tough […] I'll be glad when the Melbourne section is out of the way, because there are some sundries in the repertoire, which, once they're done, will clear the air a bit. […]

John told me that at one point he was seeing two conductors, which made life very difficult. I was preparing to fly to Australia, to meet him in Melbourne. He enclosed a list of Tips for Travellers, I having never flown such a long solo journey before.

106

From Richard Rodney Bennett
Undated, but probably 1985
(Hand-written)

No address

[…] My wind band piece is grinding along. …] I have a nice programmatic idea for it […] but all the extra instruments (E flat clt etc) are driving me nuts – I keep remembering about them & writing sudden flurries of activity after 86 bars rest. I had lunch with the nubile B. Snapp & J. Corigliano yesterday. J.C. was very nice & talked approvingly of you, so I went home & played a record of his oboe concerto […]

Am thrilled that you are doing Noctuary in Australia; second only to having you make a flying trip over to play it to me (I'll buy you a nice dinner) a cassette would be a treat. Since I remember nothing about the piece I'm sure it will all sound lovely. Sorry, that sentence is v. badly expressed. Which reminds me I'm horrified about the spelling mistake (correspondence, correspondence) & am worried it might be premature senility; when referring to A.L.W.'s major work it always comes out as REQIUEM (as well it might); […] A couple of days ago I staggered out at dawn into a heavy drizzle to go to my accountant's office to pay untold amounts of money to the I.R.S. (not one of life's more festive moments) only to find my trousers had split right up the back. I had to creep about with a very strange paralytic sideways <u>gait</u>. […] 35 productive minutes have sped by writing this & have stopped me facing the grim reality of the symphonic wind band.

Bette Snapp was the US agent of both John and Richard. John believed Noctuary, a 30-minute piece for solo piano, was a masterpiece. He recorded it twice, once in Australia and once in London, as well as performing it on numerous occasions. A copy letter from him to Richard dated May 4th 1985 enclosed a home-recorded tape cassette of his practice, and asked 13 textual questions.

From Barney Childs
5 June 85
(Typed)

Redlands,
California

[…] I have just finished an hour of – well, reading isn't quite the word, but it comes close – looking at the first issue of something called <u>Contemporary Music Review</u>, periodical out of U. of Nottingham, at least, that's where the editor-in-chief hangs out. This issue is completely devoted to "Musical Thought at IRCAM". Nice to know that musical scholarship has finally caught up with scholarship in other disciplines and has grown itself an ornate opaque pretentious prose all its very own. Apparently what happens with composers at IRCAM is that they tell the engineers what they want and the engineers then make it happen. Some nice between-the-lines grumbling about this emerges from some of the articles by the engineers. One is treated to such as this, about Boulez: "….. <u>Repons</u> of 1981, a work which seems to be the major statement of the 80's much as <u>Pli selon Pli</u> was for the 60's". Hold on there, Dominique Jameux: do you mean HIS major statement or THE major statement? The whole publication is rather like an exhumation and attempted resurrection of the <u>Die Reihe</u> volumes of 30 years ago or so. I guess all the computer capacity to make ever more complex processes available is a welcome relief to the gotta-have-the-rules people who were perhaps feeling a bit cramped now that most of the post-Webern and post-Karlheinz has been used and found old hat. And two separate reviews of the recent, I guess '84, Darmstadt point out that one of the most scurrilous terms of abuse used against certain sorts of music there was "dilettante". Ho hum. Guess I quit while I was ahead. It's a jungle out there, Major…..

[…] My new lawn, put in at great expense by a couple of Vietnamese gents (not quite sure what side they were on in the recent unpleasantness; their English is only barely better than my Vietnamese, which is nil) is growing some grass and a whole botanical garden of non-grass stuff. The gophers are finding the new crops to their liking, be sure […]

Barney fought a non-stop war against gophers on his property. Further down the letter, apropos a different topic, he writes: If you build a better mousetrap, someone will build a better mouse. It might be easy to regard Barney in musical terms as an old reactionary, but for his intelligence, and knowledge, and the fact that he was a complete 'wild man' himself. And he couldn't stand what he would have termed B……t.

John was awarded the CBE in the Queen's Birthday Honours June 1985. A flurry of congratulatory letters arrived, including from William Mathias, Denis Forman, Jane Manning and Tony Payne, Barbara Rawsthorne, Meredith Davies, James Loughran and Charles Groves.

From Richard Rodney Bennett
Dated only Aug. 23rd but almost certainly 1985
(Part typed, part hand-written)

No address

I thought you would be excited to receive a Message written on this very odd little machine which I inherited from a Friend. It does magically correct mistakes before you print them – the words come up on a teeny screen – but the general effect seems to me to suggest communications from outer space rather than the cheery, informal effect I always aim for. It would never surprise me if it suddenly started printing out messages which I had NOT typed – you are being watched, for example. [...] This machine is starting to worry me. But I am very fond of it, in a kind of nervous way, like some cute but dangerous pet. [...] What I am really writing to say was – you know how people (particularly nasty old Liz Lutyens, actually) are always talking about [...] the Creative Accident – which I am all in favour of. It stops one writing the same old piece AGAIN. WELL. I am in the middle of writing a piece for flute, viola and harp, a very pretty combination, particularly when used by C. Debussy (Americans always pronounce his name to rhyme with Q.C., which drives me mad). It's the <u>third</u> piece I've written based on Debewssy's Syrinx, which I think is probably my Favourite Piece. You can have Sheep May Safely Graze; I'll stick with Syrinx. So it was in real danger of becoming the same old piece. Well, after the obligatory scherzo (much hampered by the bloddy [*sic*] harp pedals) I was all set to write the usual R.R.B. slow movem [...]

<u>What</u>? At that point the machine went totally mad & refused to write another word. What I was saying was – I was all set to write the usual R.R.B. slow movement – Dolce Elegiaco, when (picture my astonishment) it suddenly became a demented HABAÑERA!! With glissandi <u>près de la table</u> harmonics all over the place, flutter-tongue (filth!) etc. I just wanted to share this with you. At the age of nearly 50 I have written (or am writing) my first Habañera. [...] It was nice to come back here all ready to write a lot of Real Music. As opposed to a lot of TV music, which I was doing in London – Tender is the Night, BBC TV late September. So what did I do? I fidgeted around doing absolutely <u>everything</u> but write, for three entire weeks, in frightful heat & humidity. Anyway, it's all going along now, as you will have gathered. [...]

Richard was grappling with his first word processor, computers yet on the horizon. I much prefer the character of his giant hand-writing. As a teenager, Richard had been deeply impressed by Elizabeth Lutyens, but she later turned on him, accusing him of copying her. The quarrel was eventually made up, and in her later life Richard was helpful to her. Nevertheless his feelings for her remained very ambivalent.

John to Monica
Oct. 8/86
(Hand-written)

Probably Chicago

Well, it's over – i.e. the major events. The rest is a few lectures (one on Friday) and meetings. Also a few concerts [i.e. visits to] planned, starting Friday evening here […] when I hope to see Solti. Rather a dull programme (Mendelssohn, Bach, Brahms 2) but I'm very fond of Brahms 2. I'll have a drink with Larry Coombs & I hope his wife Gail, the hornist, who went to my recital today. Which went well. It was a nice Bösendorfer, and packed house, in a wide and exceptionally handsome open hall […] & the only problems were 1) a flock of pigeons or something which in their hundreds would suddenly wheel across the windows & and block out the rather essential natural daylight!, and 2) the hiatus around when, as I discovered when nearly about to return to the stage after the opening Haydn sonata, an elderly gentleman suffered a stroke, fell down & knocked his head against a marble banister! It was decided I should go on with the show after a decent pause, & during the Ravel the man was discreetly removed by ambulance men. It is very difficult to go on and bow as usual in the circumstances, let alone play properly, but it seemed to be OK. […]

I can't remember if I told you, but last Friday a.m. in Detroit I did a live radio interview over the phone – with a repeated crossed line! (A lady who kept butting in & shouting "Hullo? Hullo?") […]

It seems to have been a rather accident-prone trip, and the letter itself is very wrinkled, as if it had received a wetting on its travels. Larry Coombs (clarinet) and his wife Gail (horn) were principals in the Chicago Symphony Orchestra. Some time later, Gail recorded John's Goddess Trilogy.

118

From David Ellis
31/10/86
(Hand-written)

Bramhall,
Cheshire.

It was kind of you to write at such a busy time. You may have seen and read the ways in which these sorry developments have escalated, via the Musicians Union, which is rather a surprise […] A large number of colleagues from every branch of the profession have deluged the BBC's Director General with letters of protest, I understand: even some to the House of Commons! The full extent is not known to me, obviously; it certainly has had an effect, for there has been <u>total</u> silence from the BBC since early September.

I have not been idle, however. Four pages of full score are completed of the "Variations upon a theme from the works of John McCabe formerly of Mount Street and other steep inclines". I would have done more but it took me 3 days to write the title page….. many thanks for your support and for your thoughts at this time.'

The 1980s were a very fractious time in many respects: The Proms and Natural Justice was published (Robert Simpson, Toccata Press) in 1981, a year after the attempt to axe the BBC orchestra in Glasgow, and the following musicians' strike. Arthur Scargill (union leader) and Ian MacGregor (representing mining and Government interests) were facing off during the turbulent Miners' Strike of the Thatcher era. Robert Simpson left the BBC (and forwent his pension by the action), while David Ellis left his position as Head of Music BBC North during this decade.

119

From the newly knighted Peter Maxwell Davies
1 March '87
(Hand-written)

Rockwick,
Hoy,
Orkney.

Many thanks for your kind letter of congratulation […] I'd like to think my being 'Sir' helps all of us trying to work creatively in music […] I hear marvellous things of your work at the College.

A brief but generous letter from Sir Peter Maxwell Davies, CBE. Conversely, when John wrote to congratulate Sir Simon Rattle on his elevation, he received a duplicated sheet in reply, despite John's family and Rattle's family knowing each other in earlier days.

120

From Simon Carrington
9/3/87
(Postcard)

Houston,
Texas.

"America Deserta" <u>great</u> success last night – many thanks from us all. It has been a challenging (!) piece to learn, but well worthwhile. 2nd performance Baltimore March 11th. [...]

Scenes in America Deserta, a prose setting named from the book by Reyner Ban-ham, was performed by the King's Singers in all their manifestations, recorded twice, and put on video. One of the singers wrote to us that it was the work they most enjoyed singing, despite the demands it made. The post-card was actually sent from Baltimore, two days later.

121

From Ursula Vaughan Williams
28th March 1987
(Hand-written)

66, Gloucester Crescent,
London NW1 7EG.

My dear John,

What a lovely surprise – thank you so much. I used to have a stamp or two in 1972, but they've gone astray – this will go directly into the 1872 file - & safety.

I had a war with the GPO – when they first showed me the proof – I explained that it was taken from a <u>rehearsal</u> photograph, that people wore tails to conduct at concerts, that they should have asked me for a proper photo if they wanted a conducting one, and that anyway, Jennifer Toombs has done much better designs, &, finally, that they'd given Ralph a sort of Baroque-bent stick instead of a baton – that one did get corrected.

It was strange to see him on a stamp - & I'm so glad that it re-emerges in part-nership with the London College. <u>Thank</u> you.'

A first-day cover had been organised by the London College of Music in connec-tion with their Centenary, and bore the Ralph Vaughan Williams stamp.

From John to Monica
May 23/87
(Hand-written)

On board flight

No hotel stationery yet, so I'm using LCM paper, & writing this on board flight to Chicago. I dare say it won't get to you until after I do, but at least I'll have written a letter! My cold is much better [...] It was a fierce, short-lived effort. Next time I do an Emanuel concert in Boston, it must be by staying at the hotel! [...] I caught the cold because of the draught & dramatic changes in temperature – the concert hall was incredibly hot but it was a very cold night [...] I nearly lost 7 shirts! I would have used the hotel laundry service, but instead had to wait till I got back to NY where I took them to a local laundry. Went to collect them on Friday, not there. Was told if they weren't there Saturday, they'd certainly be there next Tuesday (I'd asked for Friday). Anyway, to cut a long story short, I collected them on Saturday morning – plans had been laid in case of disaster (there's a shirt shop near Richard's apartment).

John writes of the Boston concert, in which he had played solo Beethoven, Ravel and Poulenc, and a Haydn Piano Trio with local musicians. He split some notes in the Beethoven, the Ravel went pretty well, and the Poulenc really well.

They finished the programme with Bartók's 6th Quartet – a good performance. Robert [Koff] of course was in the Juilliard 4-tet when they made their first, classic recording of these works, & Shannon, Bette's sister (who is becoming a very fine cellist) was very keen to learn it with the master. I still find Bartók episodic, though, despite the undoubted genius of the style & the ideas, & one of the audience said to me that though they felt they could admire the Bartók, they could really love the Poulenc. Bartók is certainly a more important composer, but how important is importance? (There's an article for "Keynote" magazine there, I think!)

[...] Went to the Juilliard Orchestra the other night – Bill Schuman 7th & Brahms 4 (no Overture!) Excellent playing [...] Schuman looks a great deal older than he did. Have heard some excellent concerts – not all music I liked (Le Marteau sans Maître sounds no better in the flesh than a din!) but all superbly played. With the Boulez went 3 works by Gerhard, & it was interesting to hear how fresh & alive they still sound (unlike the Boulez!) He really exerted a much stronger influence on me than I'd remembered, & Gemini & Libra (though not the 2nd Quartet, which is rather arid) come over with real vividness. As with all the best composers, the aural images are sharp & clear, they convey immediately not only their own content but also the composer's delight in clarifying his thoughts in this way. [...]

Shannon Snapp was the sister of Bette Snapp, who was the US agent of both John and Richard Rodney Bennett, the Richard mentioned in the letter.

123

From Anne Macnaghten
5th July 1987
(Hand-written)

23 Wymondley Rd.,
Hitchin,
Herts. SG4 9AN.

How very nice of you to write – and how amazing it is that you should remember the concert we gave for you in Manchester – so many years ago! For us it was a memorable occasion – without your invitation I don't know whether we should ever have managed to find the time to learn Bartók V – and play it many times, and for this I'm enormously grateful – such a wonderful work – and to have absorbed it must have made such an enrichment of one's musical understanding. For this I have always felt grateful to you, and have followed your career with particular interest, and have been so pleased to know of your many successes (without, I'm afraid ever writing to congratulate you). Now, thanks to your welcome letter, I can send best wishes […] We still have a quartet that functions in a limited way – 3 of us (2 violins and cello) are the same people who played for you in Manchester. Our viola (Brian Masters) has played Bartók VI with us many times, but not, alas, Bartók V.

I don't remember why John should have written to Anne Macnaghten, but he was in close contact with Iris Lemare, who with Anne had started the Macnaghten-Lemare concerts so many years earlier. John as a student in Manchester organised concerts for the Manchester Institute of Contemporary Arts. Another of his concerts starred Peter Pears and Benjamin Britten, for whom he page-turned, noting Britten's acute nervousness. It is strange that in this book Anne Macnaghten's encomium for Bartók should coincidentally follow the mild strictures in John's letter to me.

From Beryl Bainbridge
11.8.87
(Typed)

42 Albert Street,
London NW1.

It was lovely to get your note – and what a pity we missed each other. I have followed <u>your</u> career and am equally pleased that you have done so well, though in your case there was never any doubt. I always remember that lovely painting that Aussie did of you when you were a little boy in short pants. He lives in New Zealand and I haven't seen him in fifteen years, but he is coming to see the children in October this year. Remember me to your mother.

John had written to Beryl Bainbridge to congratulate her on her Dame-hood. He knew her, and her then husband, Austin Davies, from the years when they lived in the basement flat in the house of Gordon Green, his piano teacher in Liverpool. Beryl Bainbridge was then an actress, while her husband was an artist, and some-time scene-painter. He did a portrait of John, aged about twelve.

From Christopher Gunning
30th August 1987
(Hand-written)

The Old Rectory,
Mill Lane,
Monks Risborough,
Bucks. HP17 9LG.

Nicholas and I tried to find you after your piece was played at the prom the other evening – but couldn't. And every time I've tried to phone you since I've got the engaged signal – presumably you've been inundated with fans ringing up to congratulate you!

Your piece is magnificent! I am lost in admiration. The colours throughout are wonderfully imaginative – and I've never heard a brass band sounding like that. Everything "came off" beautifully, from the quite lovely evocative bits to the bombastic, exhilarating sections. It has a sense of purpose right from the word go, and is consistently interesting – the brass (& percussion) writing is simply stupendous. It must be the most significant addition to the brass band repertory for years and years. I loved the harmonic sense that is <u>always</u> such a feature of your music [...]

So, in other words, "Well done" and 11/10, even though I gather you didn't do all the transpositions yourself (well, why <u>should</u> tubas play in the treble clef?)

Thank you for the Copland, which I've still got & will return [...] In the event, my "statements" about Epstein ranged from a short Messiaen rip-off to a bit of ragtime. I <u>still</u> don't know what music <u>really</u> goes with his sculptures, but I did do a bit of pseudo, and rather basic, Copland for one bit, and that proved to be the bit that the director liked best. So, thank you!

Certainly a fan letter to dream of. The brass band work would have been Cloud-catcher Fells. Chris Gunning and John became very friendly through working for the Association of Professional Composers, and via the Performing Right Society, the latter not pleasing classical composers, especially at that time. Christopher was then working mainly for television and advertising, but has since written numerous symphonies.

126

From Anthony Hodges
5 October 1987
Typed)

As from
The Alan Rawsthorne Society

We all enjoyed the concert here at the RNCM last Friday very much and, on behalf of the Society, I wish to extend to you our great appreciation and gratitude for your generous contribution. The Sonatina has not been heard here before and everyone was so impressed by its energy and the lucid account you gave. [...]

This was I believe the first meeting of the recently formed Alan Rawsthorne Society, at the Royal Northern College of Music in Manchester. Anthony Hodges had taken the position of Secretary.

127

From Aulis Sallinen
31.12.87
(Typed)

Finland

Dear Mr Cabe,

I thank you warmly for your kind letter as well as for the tape. It was a great pleasure to listen to both works: the lucky interpretation of my symphony – performed by your youthful orchestra – and before all your powerful 3rd symphony. There is an especial reason to be happy about the fact that the symphonic form is still alive and there are composers – as you – who still believe in it. In the spring I met James Stobart and he told me that several pieces of mine have been performed there. It is very important, since we know that contemporary works in generally are not too often played. The activity of your orchestra gives the young musician an idea of the gramma [*sic*] of new music: a very promising perspective! [...]

I reproduce this charming letter from Aulis Sallinen as it is written. It was addressed to Mr Cabe, at the London College of Music, where John had instituted a Scandinavian Music Year. James Stobart was a frequent conductor of the College orchestra, and John (who greatly admired Sallinen's music) was very insistent on the performance of contemporary works. Many people, not only abroad but also in the UK, had trouble with John's name. As a student in Germany his correspondence was always filed under C for Cabe. It goes without saying that Mr Sallinen's English was far more fluent than John's Finnish.

128

From Alun Hoddinott
January 7 1988
(Hand-written)

Maesawelon,
86 Mill Rd.,
Lisvane,
Cardiff CF4 5UG.

I still feel disappointed at missing the performance of "Heaventree of Stars" – I do hope that all went well and the soloist enjoyed playing the piece [...] Anyway, many thanks for putting it on [...]

Another contemporary work at the London College of Music. Alun Hoddinott wrote many notes to John, usually very brief and very seldom dated.

129

From Derek Bourgeois
12/4/88
(Hand-written)

The Vines,
Hewelsfield,
Lydney,
Glos. GL15 6XE.

Thank you so much for your wonderful contribution to the NYO course. You were so calm and helpful during the various crises that one almost forgot to realise what a remarkable standard of performance that you yourself were giving. I think the concerto itself is super, and your own playing masterly. […]

The "Infernal Machine" is sensational, and I very much hope that I can find a slot for it soon. […]

The National Youth Orchestra, at that time run by Derek, had a major crisis for this Easter course. The engaged conductor was taken ill, and Peter Stark took the course over at 24 hours' notice, including learning John's massive Third Piano Concerto, which John himself was performing. Peter coped superbly with the challenge. John had obviously recommended 'The Infernal Machine' by the American composer Christopher Rouse, to Derek for another NYO course, but I do not know if this happened.

130

From Ursula Vaughan Williams
19ᵗʰ November 1988
(Hand-written)

London NW1

I see that you, too, have written a Stabat Mater. Ralph was planning to conduct Dvořák's – at one of the Leith Hill Festivals - & set me the task of making a translation – rather a daunting one with our lack of feminine endings – so I did it – and he didn't – because, as I remember, there are several pages of the choir singing fac, fac, fac (& fac again) in verse five & you can imagine how that came out…..anyway, I do think that most translations, though you may have found a good one, are rather dull – so I venture to send you mine (the Bach Choir have used it) for the programme, should you like it. […]

John replied, 1st December 1988, accepting her translation with pleasure, and fully understanding RVW's reasons for not in the end performing the work. He informs her that he noticed that Dona Nobis Pacem was advertised for performance in New York when he was there.

From Edward and Joan Downes
Jan. 19th 1989
(Hand-written, probably by Joan)

7, Kidbrooke Gardens,
Blackheath,
London SE3 0PD.

[…] We did enjoy last Friday. What could be better, a splendid concert and a dinner to celebrate. The concert in Leeds went well, with a repeat of Helden-leben in a very different acoustic. I look forward to hearing your "Fire" music again in Prague. We had a fire in Leeds, too – obviously the spell was still work-ing. You <u>must</u> come to Prague.

Edward (Ted) Downes had just premiered John's Fire at Durilgai with the BBC Philharmonic Orchestra in Manchester, 13th January 1989, with a follow-up con-cert in Leeds. We had sent the Downes flowers. Fire at Durilgai was performed in Prague, in a memorable concert in May, with the BBC PO conducted by Downes. This was before the Berlin Wall came down. Beautiful Prague was looking very shabby. There were Russian soldiers in evidence, and the shops were empty of goods.

132

From Nicholas Maw
23rd April 89
(Hand-written)

Washington DC 20012

Thank you so much for sending the notices, though in fact I did manage to catch a glimpse of this lot […] before I left. I was completely surprised by the out and out rave from Michael John White. […] Most of the other dailies seemed to be treading very cautiously […] I don't think they are very comfortable dealing with a piece that obviously can't be summed up (or decimated!) in a few words. I was very sorry that so few of them wrote about the concert in the afternoon which contained superlative performances; […]

Maw's Odyssey for orchestra, a work of musical gigantism lasting non-stop for 96 minutes, which had taken some 15 years to write, had just received its first com-plete performance, although there had previously been a partial performance at the Proms. The Royal Festival Hall was not full for the performance, but it was swarming with composers.

From Nicholas Maw
14th June 1989
(Typed)

Washington DC 20012

[…] A nice piece on your birthday from Ted Greenfield, John – though I was unaware that Hitchcock was the director of Rio Bravo. I was also unaware that you had a habit of falling in the fire as a child; it's probably a good thing that the whole country is now a smokeless zone […] I hadn't put two and two together and made the connection that we were both having works played in the Prague Spring Festival (as a matter of fact, I didn't realise the Prague performance of Spring Music was going to <u>be</u> in a festival) until you sent me the programme, Monica. (For which many thanks – and, no, nobody else had sent me a copy.) […] You mentioned the BBCPO 'played very well' for my concert. Did they not do so for John's? I was very sorry indeed to miss that occasion […] I was chained to my desk getting pieces done for the Lichfield Festival. One was a set of Three Hymns for SATB and organ for the cathedral choir and the other a large-scale work for solo guitar entitled Music of Memory. […]The trouble about writing for either the organ or guitar is that in the end you only write 'organ music' or 'guitar music' – if you catch my drift.

For the cathedral concert you, John, have done the very charitable (or fool-hardy) thing of putting yourself at the blunt end of a beginner conductor. I realise this could put our friendship to a severe test. […] I don't know whether you know, but I have also agreed to conduct (?) the BBCPO in Spring Music <u>the next day</u> (as it turns out), with a rehearsal <u>in Manchester</u> on the day of our concert. Two further points are relevant here: a) Spring Music turns out to be very difficult and b) I have never conducted an orchestra in my life before. It is a very good thing they had a chance this spring to learn the piece thoroughly with Ted Downes while on tour. <u>They</u> are going to have to teach it to <u>me</u>. […]

The BBCPO performed John's Fire at Durilgai brilliantly also, and it went down extraordinarily well with the audience, some of whom I think connected it with their own war-time experiences, and were slightly disappointed to find that it related only to a literary wild-fire in Australia – though who knows what relevance it had for John and his own childhood fire experience.

134

From Barney Childs
Monday 19 June 1989
(Typed)

Redlands,
California

[…] I'm working, if such it can be called, on the commissioned tympani concerto, and the process is rather like do-it-yourself dentistry. After two minutes of tympani playing, what do you do for pleasing and surprising the ear? I suppose I'll get it done, but it isn't going to be a Milestone. […] As a final encouragement [*to John, to visit*] I shall mention the international viola conference which begins here later this week. I'm sure you have heard all the viola jokes, but the imminence of 300 violists at the University is a new one. Perhaps I will find I have sudden business which requires my presence elsewhere – like maybe Ulan Bator.…

Violists are sadly the butt of many jokes, often by violinists.…..

135

From Stuart Robinson
28 July 1989
(Typed)

Halle Concerts Society,
30 Cross Street,
Manchester M2 7BA.

Thanks for your kind letters of 16 July to both Clive [*Smart*] and myself. I write to acknowledge both as Clive went on the German Tour and I didn't. This means that Clive has gone on holiday to lie down in a dark room! I write this letter on the Friday of the Test when the news is that we are all out for 260 and they are 73 for no wicket. So, I'm heading for a darkened room! I'm going to Old Trafford [*cricket ground*] tomorrow and I think there's nothing else for it but for me to do a streak! […]

So far, so good re the hall. I understand that we're down to a short list of consortia; that the building of the hall will be "acoustics led", as opposed to "architect led". These are two very "in" phrases. Nevertheless, you'll get the idea. We've all submitted our views – written and orally – on the Concert Hall of our dreams. So have the BBC, Granada [*TV*], Manchester Camerata, etc. So far everybody refers to the hall as the Halle Orchestra's home – with our offices, music library etc. […] In the meantime, keep smiling – it's the West Indies this winter.'

Stuart Robinson was for very many years Orchestral Manager of the Halle orchestra. The new hall, named the Bridgewater Hall, after the notable who built the nearby Bridgewater Canal of the Industrial Revolution, turned out to be a complete success. The West Indies cricket team at that time were regarded as the most formidable international side, with both fearsome fast bowlers and magnificent batsmen. John and Stuart shared a deep love and knowledge of cricket.

136

From Ann Bond (Avery)
16/08/89
(Hand-written)

Godstone,
Surrey.

Listening to "Fire at Durilgai" on last night's Prom, I was greatly impressed by its imaginative power & am writing to congratulate you warmly – if that's not the wrong word! – on a fine piece. I have always secretly taken a little credit for the fact that I pointed out the promise of your composition – on a very brief inspection – to HPG when he was all set to reject your application to the M/er Music department. Getting in there was probably, with hindsight, something of a mixed blessing! but I hope at least you do not cherish as bitter memories as "Max". Some of us, at least, were doing our best in far from ideal conditions.

Having brought up my family - an electronic engineer & an environmental ecologist! – I am now establishing myself as a professional harpsichordist, which I much enjoy. C17-C18 is and always was my favourite period: I don't always get on well with contemporary music, though there are honourable exceptions! […]

I'm not sure who Ann Bond (Avery) was, having never to my knowledge met her, but presumably she taught at Manchester University. HPG, as Humphrey Procter-Gregg was usually known, was the composition professor with whom John crossed swords, and then moved to the Royal Manchester College of Music. Clearly Peter Maxwell Davies experienced the same lack of empathy.

1990–1994

137

From Thea Musgrave
January 4 1990
(Typed)

c/o Virginia Opera Association,
Norfolk,
Virginia 23501.

First of all a very happy New Year….I hope it will be a good one for all of us composers!

Anyway, I'm writing because I heard from Bette Snapp that you are planning a visit to our shores shortly. As you perhaps know I am now teaching at Queens College in New York and one of the things I do is organise a COMPOSERS' WORKSHOP. This means I can invite friends to come and talk about their music! The bad thing is that I only have a really tiny budget. (New York is, as usual, in a state of financial crisis!) And so I can only offer you the paltry sum of $100. However it would be really nice for the students to get to meet you….. The meetings are always on a MONDAY and start at 7.30pm and end at about 9.30pm. What I propose is to meet up in Manhattan round about 4.30-5, go out to Flushing together by public transport, invite you to partake of a Chinese meal (there's a fabulous restaurant there!) and then I would bring you back to the city in a slightly more elegant way (limo!). Well, does this appeal? I would be delighted if you can. […]

138

From Richard Rodney Bennett
Dated only August 28 but almost certainly 1990
(Hand-written)

No address

I'm beside myself about your recording of Noctuary – what a good idea. All kinds of good luck with the recording; the idea of doing the Copland <u>and</u> Carter the same week + Adams is mind-boggling. I've had a very nice time since my return, just <u>writing music.</u> I was asked by Canterbury Cathedral to do a Mass (moan, groan) in English. Felt absolutely guilty & said yes, but was horrified by the English text, like setting the small print of a contract, said sorry & felt relieved. So they said Never Mind, set it in Latin. So all of a sudden I did, and had a good time, & like the result, full of cheerful but decorous tunes. Then out of the blue I had a call from John Williams (comp. not guit.) who had been discussing with Stan Getz (the world's greatest jazz tenor sax. as you know) the idea of a concerto for him with perhaps the Boston Pops. J.W. told S. G. that I was the only composer capable of doing it (which may or may not be true, [...] certainly I'm the only composer capable of writing a cheerful Mass and then a concerto for S.G.) [...] Since then the whole thing has got quite out of hand: Bette Snapp has asked an ASTRONOMICAL fee & the premiere will be in the spring, probably at the HOLLYWOOD BOWL. In the meantime I'm happily writing it – my first cross-over piece, strings & timps only.

As you know, I'm not given to boasting about commissions, fees, etc (God is likely to punish one very swiftly) but I thought it would amuse you..... Afterwards it's back to symphonic <u>wind</u> ensemble (moan, groan).

I have some very good jokes (one involving a shipwreck a dog & a flock of sheep) but would be arrested if I put them in a letter. [...]

Love to you both from me both, R.

PS Good luck with the Flute Concerto!

From Monica to John, in Australia
20/1/91
Hand-written)

Southall

It's Monday morning, just after 9am, & I'm waiting for the bloke to turn up to mend the kitchen window. Since I don't know any way to hurry up a workman's appointment other than to start to do something else, I thought I'd spend the time by writing you a letter. [...] Obviously we have spoken at great length & enormous expense about most of the important things, so this is really just a jotting about peripheral matters. [...] I am really quite amazingly glad we have reached this point in time, with all the most important problems behind us. I don't know how you've managed to cope with the stress & worry of it all [...] I do now, in a way feel that that whole area of our lives is behind us, despite still wanting to see the LCM affair properly settled, & financially secure, for our own pride's sake as much as anything else. [...]

People have been very kind since you left, & I've had quite a few phone calls […] Indeed the time has passed amazingly quickly. […] Most days I work, one way or the other, most of the day, starting maybe around 10am & only taking time off for preparation of meals, perhaps a bit of crossword; sometimes something on TV, and then on till 11am [*sic – pm!*] or more.

The other distraction is of course the war – which we've already discussed on the phone. The blow-by-blow account on news & teletext, is extraordinarily addictive, & although I have a few qualms about the voyeuristic nature of the "entertainment", I have felt extraordinarily sober, sombre and non-jingoistic about the affair. Two little illustrative gems of nationality to pass on, however. One is Jewish, in a phone interview with someone or other in Tel Aviv, as they were being, what do you say "missiled". He was asked some dam fool question about how did he feel about being sealed up in a shuttered room with his family. He replied spontaneously, "What do you mean? This is quality time with my family. We are not often so much together." I thought that was pretty good in the circumstances.

The other was illustrative of chipper British phlegm. An interview, this time with pictures, with a stocky, ginger-haired, balding ground-crew bomb-loader, a Londoner I should think. Again he was asked some dam fool question along the lines of what did he think about the success of the bombing missions. He replied briskly and cheerfully, "Well it makes my job worthwhile a bit, dunnit! I put 'em on, they take 'em off'. (Aside) "Got a screw-driver?" […]

Well, there was a very long pause at this point, as young Mr Allbright Glass has finished the window (& seems to have done a nice job), & so I have been paying & chatting about the Gulf War, on which he appears to hold highly intelligent & sensible views, as they coincide entirely with my own. Indeed, like me, he sat up late into the night on the first two nights, following events - & to speak seriously, his views do appear sombre, realistic & well-balanced, especially about the possibility of a major conflagration if Israel does enter the War. […]

A rare, surviving letter from me. I seldom wrote to John while he was away, because I could not be sure that letters would reach him before he moved on. John had just left the London College of Music, and almost immediately travelled to Australia. The College had been very unhappy and divided over the move to Ealing, which was however necessary on economic grounds, and the unsuitability of the central London building. The turbulence in the Middle East had exploded into the Gulf War, about which again there was much dissension in Britain. I also informed John about the death of A. Wainwright, who wrote a classic series of guide books to the Lake District, which were of great interest to him.

From John to Monica
Jan. 30/91
(Hand-written)

Australia, probably Melbourne

Thank you for your letter, which arrived yesterday! At least it arrived – I was beginning to wonder if it had been put in one of the other post-boxes. […] The night before last I had to get up at 3a.m., put on shorts, shoes and a raincoat, take my umbrella & go into the backyard & deal (successfully, or pretty so) with the gate which is, as it were, directly behind my head when asleep. […] It […] drags noisily back & forth when buffeted by strong winds. I picked up a handy brick & tried to wedge it – not necessarily wise, since picking up a brick without knowing what is under them is generally frowned upon. However, all was well, & since the temperature was still c. 70 I did not catch cold. […]

I'm taking a break before getting back to work on rounding off the wind band piece, which is very near completion. Today, with luck, will see it complete, & I can send it off tomorrow. […] Frid. a.m. I looked at the piano for the Ravel, Mon. a.m. I do my interval talk on Ravel & on the influence of French music on English music (eh?). Notice seen in the "common room" (ie green room for concerts) at the National Gallery: "Owing to unforeseen circumstances, the coffee bar will open next week". […]

The Gulf War must have seemed far away, but the ABC radio Test Match commentary was interrupted apparently at random, every 10 minutes or so, for 'the latest Gulf update', adds John.

John and Monica feed wild parakeets at a picnic spot in the rainforest area known as the Dandenongs, outside Melbourne. Probably 1991. 140

141

From Andre Previn to Bette Snapp, who faxed it on
June 2 1991
(Typed)

No address

Yesterday I received the new John McCabe CD which you were kind enough to send me. It came as a complete surprise. I didn't even know that John was aware of that particular set of piano pieces from 1974. Of course I played the record immediately, and am full of admiration for the playing. […] I don't have any sort of current address or phone for him; would you do me a great favour and tell him how much I liked the record and how much I appreciate his having taken the piece on. […]

This was the 2-CD set previously mentioned, with Richard Rodney Bennett's Noctuary, Carter, Copland, and Previn's set of piano pieces entitled The Invisible Drummer, recorded by Continuum.

142

From Stephen Oliver
Undated, but c. 1991
(Postcard)

No address

What a wonderful letter to get. I'm bowled over: thank you so much for taking the trouble. Praise from a fellow-worker outweighs all the bad reviews in the world. I'm really touched and grateful. It was a very <u>comforting</u> thing to do. Ever love to you both.

Stephen was very sick with AIDS. His opera, Timon of Athens [ENO 1991] had just been mauled by the Press. It had been given a dull production, seemingly low-budget. John disagreed with the Press, and wrote Stephen a letter of praise. Stephen died in April 1992.

From John to The Times
9/7/91
(Typed)

Southall

If Mr. H. A. (letter, July 3) selects concerts "carefully to avoid any piece of a non-melodic nature", and does not listen to Radio 3 without, presumably, selecting programmes for listening according to the same principle, how on earth does he know what is and is not of a non-melodic nature?

144

To Barney Childs
August 3/91
(Typed)

Southall

Well now. It is some time since I wrote to you, indeed I believe it must be well over a year, during which time a lot has happened. I'm in the throes of catching up with a lot of correspondence, much of which has accumulated during the 7 years of my administrative labours (which left precious little time for the social niceties or indeed, in some cases, nasties) – I have now, during two bursts of letter-writing (with another few days to go) replied to at least three letters dated 1989.

I have to hand yours of June last year, so I suspect you are out of your turn and have jumped the queue, but your news of taking the pledge is so serious that strong action is required. I trust you have been able to keep up to this promise, and that marrow bone samples have not been necessitated. Phil [*Rehfeldt*] sent me a tape of Part 2 of the Great Clarinet Marathon, which was an extraordinary achievement and splendidly played throughout – you got some nice pieces in your Festschrift, too, I thought. Liked Maslanka's Little Symphony – now there's a labour-saving work, which gives rise to thought (perhaps one could, without too much trouble, beat Havergal Brian and get to the really big-time – Mozart, maybe even Haydn?).

As I say, a lot has been happening. I left the College at the end of December, putting my departure forward by 7 months, the reason being a trip to Australia which lasted from January 10 to c. April 12 this year – the clash of priorities the offer to make this trip represented was inevitable, and I suppose it is surprising it didn't happen sooner, but of course if it came to having to choose between music and administration, there was really no contest. I am lucky to be able to have a good reason for leaving music education, which in this country is in a parlous state and requires full-time fighters at the moment, to fight the good fight. So I left, and the College will actually be situated in Ealing (they rather piously hope) – a very good deal, which I did initiate, and which offers them terrific security for the future.

While in Australia I wrote three pieces (one finished when I got back), and have since done another, a short choral work for the William Ferris Chorale in Chicago which will be in their 20th anniversary concert at the end of next March. A lot more to do in the next couple of months, and some recordings (of British stuff, mostly), as well as a few concerts. Australia was fun, but very hard work – 5 concertos (all classical), some recitals, and a month's residency at Melbourne University. I stayed in Melbourne most of the time, with a few side trips, and Monica joined me for March, when I had my one and only day off – we went with some friends to the Dandenongs (rainforest area in the mountains near Melbourne) and needless to say it rained, which was quite exceptional for this trip.

Getting back here, I've been plunged into a pretty wide variety of work. I did 2 ½ weeks on the jury of a new piano competition in London – very high-powered and rather enjoyable, with none of the traumas which reputedly occur within juries on such occasions. Rather a lot of Chopin, which I like very much when it lasts c. 9 minutes, but not so much when it is either shorter or longer. Also quite a lot of Rachmaninov, which I love anyway except for the 2nd Sonata, which, wouldn't you know, we got more of than any other major work. There was some good playing, and the thing got off to a good start. I'm still not convinced about such things, but in this case there was a real attempt to organise the repertoire so that people didn't play all the same obvious pieces all the time and had to think about their programming. They still found ways round the list to do the usual things, but sooner or later they were FORCED to think, and this has to be good.….

So here I am, catching up with a mountain of letters, planning my next piece (which is for 13 wind instruments, and they want a contrabassoon instead of the double-bass that for some reason is customary), and not really thinking much further ahead. Incidentally, one of the recent pieces was a wind-band piece called Canyons (Richard Rodney Bennett suggested my next piece should be called Stars, or preferably Etoiles), which I'll try to remember to send you when I have a tape of it. This was done a couple of weeks or so ago, and I sandwiched a quick trip to Istanbul, no less, between the two performances. I merely mention this in passing to impress you, since my only other trip this year is likely to be to Manchester. Can you tell me why double-bass (which I didn't use in this one either) is deemed so essential to wind groups? I am, by the way, still awaiting a tape of your Timpani concerto and the one for English horn.

148

From Angela Simpson
4th February 1992
(Typed)

Siochain,
Killelton, Camp, Tralee,
Co. Kerry, Eire.

[…] No, Bob won't be doing the Ruislip date [*Gramophone society lecture*] […] His mobility has improved a little but he is still in a lot of pain which is apparently rare and difficult to treat. We see the neurologist tomorrow and I just hope that he will be able to recommend something that will give him some relief. We are coming to England for Simon Rattle's concert in the RFH on 12th February when he is doing Bob's No. 9. Ray Few is being wonderful and fixing up access for wheelchair etc. I think the journey is going to be very tiring for Bob but, on the whole, I hope the occasion will do him more good than harm. […]

John and I attended this concert, and saw Bob and Angela there. A kind Irish neighbour who came with them to help with the travel appeared somewhat bemused by Bob's symphony. Ray Few was well-known in the music world, and was I believe at that time associated with the Royal Philharmonic Society. Sadly Bob did continue to suffer pain from his stroke for the rest of his life.

149

From William Mathias
5/4/92
(Hand-written)

Anglesey.

A <u>thousand thanks</u> for your kind and thoughtful letter of March. Perhaps you can gauge my attitude to things from the fact that the slight delay in replying is due to the fact that I've been occupied by two (perhaps three) new pieces! […] The new little local difficulty revealed itself (quite suddenly) at the turn of the year, & yes, my medicos forbade me America – to which I had been so looking forward. They were, of course, right, but it was <u>hugely</u> frustrating to miss the Ferris concert (which I have on tape) & events in NY and Boston (including the "Celtic Dances" by the Boston Symphony). I find US trips very invigorating not least because they take you as you are. But time wasn't wasted – I finished a Flute Concerto for Wib Bennett, to be premiered in June.

Oddly I find in this situation that the creative fires are if anything stronger & much more concentrated – there have certainly been three big pieces (Symphony 3, Vln. Concerto, "In Arcadia") as good as anything I've done. […] Yvonne and Rhiannon are wonderfully supportive […] I really am most grateful for your splendid, good and friendly wishes, & assure you that if I can conquer this damn thing I will! […]

Sadly he died three months later, in July 1992, with his Fourth Symphony unfinished. Yvonne and Rhiannon were wife and daughter respectively. The William Ferris Chorale was a large and influential choir in Chicago. John also worked with them on a number of occasions.

150

From Yvonne Mathias
14/7/92
(Hand-written)

Anglesey.

I thank you both for your letters. The support and affection gave me much comfort. Will's positive attitude over the last months gave <u>me</u> courage. We decided not to waste one precious moment. He worked until the very last day. […]

151

John to Monica
18/03/1992
(Postcard)

This gives no idea of how impressive this picture really is! Went to see Monet's "Water Lilies" again – worth the trip just for that. The Verdehr Trio commission is on for July 93. Various people send greetings and love […]

The postcard picture was Magritte's The Empire of Light, from the Museum of Modern Art, New York. The Verdehr Trio commission was Fauvel's Rondeaux, written in 1996 and premiered July 8 1997 Michigan State University. I do not now recall what the considerable delay was for.

152

John to Monica
Possibly 26th March 1992
(Postcard)

It's a good thing you didn't know about the 2 planes that went off the runway here on Saturday night! Practising is going well, & life is not too hectic. I hope the recital goes well, & that I arrive on time! […]

Another postcard from the Museum of Modern Art, this time a Seurat, but posted elsewhere. Presumably snowstorms were the problem. As with the postcard above, the date is difficult to be certain of.

153

From David Bintley
7th August 1992
(Hand-written)

3 Cranborne Road,
Muswell Hill,
N10 2BT.

Our mutual friend, Paul Reade, who wrote my ballet "Hobson's Choice", recently said to me that you might be interested in our collaborating. […] I have long been an admirer of "Notturni ed Alba", "Chagall Windows" and "Hartmann Variations" as well as the 1st Symphony. Does your publisher have any recent works on tape? There is a criminal lack of them on commercial recordings. […]

Sadly the criminal lack still applies…..

154

To David Bintley
September 2/92
(Typed)

Southall

[…] I've taken my time replying because you were away on holiday, but I was really delighted to hear from you. Yes, I would certainly be keen to collaborate on a ballet […] I'm very grateful to Paul Reade for passing on the remark that

I'd like to work with you – I thought that "Hobson's Choice" was terrific, musically and otherwise, and am very glad it has been so successful. [...]

So began a correspondence which changed the course of John's composing career for many years. Hobson's Choice, incidentally, has been one of David Bintley's most successful ballets.

155

From David Bintley
Early October 1992
(Hand-written)

Muswell Hill

Many thanks for the tapes, which I am enjoying tremendously. I'm very busy commuting to Birmingham, working with the Royal Ballet there, [...] but hope to meet with you possibly in early November.

156

From David Bintley
Undated, but c. 1992/3
(Hand-written)

No address

Here is a scenario based on Marlowe's "Ed. II", which it's taken me a couple of years to complete and for which I'd like you to write the music. I saw the R.S.C. [Royal Shakespeare Company] production two years ago and didn't like it much – they'd lost the humanity of Ed. and Isabella by trying to shock; it's shocking enough anyway! I read the play later tho' as the characters stayed in my mind and the stark realities and certainties of that period (making for beautiful, if brutal images) seemed to me rich ground for dance theatre. Later I saw Derek Jarman's film which though visually arresting I felt was just a homosexual tract; the "updating" of events detracting from the fact that this "domestic drama" in reality brought about not one but two civil wars in our country, the catastrophic defeat at Bannockburn and the worst period of government England had ever seen. A bit hard to believe when Jarman substituted the vicious and terrifying "Marcher" and "Ordainer" Lords with a bunch of Mrs Whitehouse look-alike Tories! (I do believe there are parallels with our times. But not such specific ones.)

What <u>does</u> interest me about Ed. II though is essentially this play between "chamber" drama – super concentrated emotional moments of often (obviously) unusual character – and the dramatic repercussions which result in large-scale movements – the Civil War, the invasion by Isabella's forces – scenes of obsequies and coronation.

Not written into the scenario is an idea I have for threading a series of perhaps not too obviously related scenes based on the "Jongleur" or "Minnesinger" idea – Seven Deadly Sins or The Wheel of the Ages of Man. I have a picture (supposedly based on the Mediaeval Wheel, and Ed. II's fortunes) which shows a man becoming King, losing crown, etc. "Regnabo, regno, regnavi; sum sine regno" . It might be interesting to fleck this often grim canvas with a bit of genuine mediaeval sound and colour! I have a few recordings, (Carmine Veris et Amoris; Carmina Moralia et Divina etc.) of "authentic" Carmina Burana which I like very much. Perhaps a vocal element would not come amiss. However, having said all this it is essentially the characters and their individual plights that move me, particularly Edward and Isabella. They are both despicable, but deserving of compassion, both trapped in roles they were unable to fulfil according to the times. Both transgressed the law of "courtly love" by their respective homosexuality and adultery and, on discovery, paid the price. […] The final image of Edward's terrible death and the last encounter with his torturer – the almost abstract Lightborn; the pitiless avenging angel/Demon, almost excuse and pardon the ex-King's sins. It is no wonder he was later venerated as a Saint!

Hope this strikes a chord!

It did, and unlike that of Edward and Isabella, proved to be a marriage made in heaven, between David's almost fully-formulated (at this point) conception of the ballet, and John's realisation of the score – though in the end no vocal element, nor actual mediaeval music were used by John.

157

From James Loughran
5 February 93
(Hand-written)

The Rookery,
Bollington Cross,
Macclesfield.

Your letter caught up with me in Montpellier where I conduct Mahler 9 tonight. The environment for music making here is perfect. Town of 200,000 or so inhabitants – University – public pack the hall for every concert and there's a lot of music. Opera House – new concert hall (2000) and a splendid orchestra which organised de la Grange to come and give a lecture last week on the Mahler and offered me 10 rehearsals. Posters everywhere – flower stalls, car-park, restaurants etc. and both performances (tonight & tomorrow) sold out. Next week we do Schubert Bartòk Martucci! I went slightly crazy this season taking on a bit too much and all different programmes – I don't stop until mid-August – if I survive! However last summer I drew up repertoires for the next four seasons that I would offer to various orchestras (16 this season!) and I'm pleased to say your works were there (before I received your letter!) and from a greatly reduced list. Selling them is a different matter and here the director is Rene Koering – a composer from the Boulez school.

However, I hope we will be able to meet before either of us attend each other's memorial service! May this year bring all that you wish. […]

A happy and generous-hearted letter from James (Jimmie) Loughran, who seems well-settled following the palace revolution at the Halle in 1983, when he, the Chief Executive and Concerts Manager were all changed, although the last was brought back on the staff as he was found to be indispensible. Henry-Louis de la Grange was a French musicologist.

158

From Richard Rodney Bennett
4/05/93
(Typed and faxed)

No address

[…] I should be honoured if you wanted to write variations on any theme of mine, except perhaps the main title from Murder on the you-know-what. Sonnets to Orpheus would be fine, tho' perhaps the opening of the 3rd Symphony would be even better. That is my favourite piece, and I've been writing variations on it ever since…..The opening tune is more compact and has a very nice shape; the beginning of S. to O. depends an awful lot on the accompanying texture – see M.B.W.'s Tpt. Concerto.

I shouldn't be writing this; I should be practising the Dutilleux oboe sonata, which I have to accompany very soon, or alternatively the piano part of my own "After Syrinx" for the same concert, which I make the most terrible mess of. The other day I said, quite spontaneously, in rehearsal, "Thank God the composer isn't here!" Or then again I should be doing a million small tedious things which have to be done before I leave for GLASGOW tomorrow, for a joyful festival of contemporary music (my favourite thing). Then I shall be in London for a trice, arriving on the 9th for the glittering premiere (pronounced preMEER) of my bassoon sonata. […]

I am in the middle of a concerto for trumpet and the dread symph. wind band, not a very nice combination. I don't know if it's any good yet. As far as the inspiration flowing with ease, which you so kindly suggest, I haven't written anything since LAST JUNE, not a thought in my head. It will be followed by a very jazzy ten-min. piano piece, which you may play […]

Sadly John's idea for variations on a theme of Richard's did not materialise. Neither I think did John ever play the 'very jazzy piano piece'. M.B.W. was Michael Blake Watkins.

159

To Barney Childs
May 13/93
(Typed)

Southall

[…] we also became extremely exotic, got up at 3.30a.m. (which, contrary to my belief is a time which does exist after all) and drove (through thick fog) to Oxford in order to hear the May Madrigals sung from the top of Magdalen Tower at Dawn. (Capitals are catching.) All went well, and the street was thronged with happy (merry, perhaps, would be a better word) students wearing evening dress which, in my innocence, I believed they normally wore to breakfast. Madrigals were duly sung. The only intimation we had that it had really occurred was the pealing of the bells, which happened three times, getting louder each time – the first time was more of an exercise in cluster chords than a peal of bells. We learnt that this signified that the madrigals had been sung.

Fortunately Monica discovered that they were going to do another bout because a film crew up there in the mist with them wanted another take, and she powered us into the Magdalen College quad, so we heard distant snatches of a couple of catchy numbers before going off and having an excellent breakfast. […]

I haven't done much writing since, at the cost of much effort, I finally finished my big piano piece – this is a piece for big piano, naturally. It took a lot of work, and rather exhausted me […] A lot of work to do, though, including a symphony which has only taken 2 and a half years for the commission to be agreed, thanks to the work of 3 people in Australia, my ex-agent here, my publishers, 2 people at the BBC, and myself. It was all sorted out when I finally lost patience and waded politely in with suggestions that it must be terribly frustrating for every-body not to be able to complete the deal and might I propose that we did just that. It took about two weeks then. […]

The big piano work was John's Tenebrae, often regarded as his piano masterwork. The symphony was No. 4, Of Time and the River, a co-commission between the BBC SO and the Melbourne SO. The fog, throughout the journey to Oxford, was so bad as to be quite frightening. Had I known it would last all 40 miles from West London I would have turned back. Because it was so dense it dampened the sound of singing from the tower, rendering it inaudible. The film crew was filming for the film Shadowlands, about the love affair between C. S. Lewis and Joy Davidman.

160

From John to Monica
October 19 and 24 1993
(Hand-written)

Australia

[…] It has been a very interesting trip. Port Fairy was splendid, a lovely little village & a real Festival atmosphere. I got two of the biggest audiences (for the 2 Haydn events) & it all went very well. Carl Pini's new quartet made an excellent debut & played my No. 3 superbly, I thought […] I was driven from Mount Gambier to Port Fairy & back again by a winery family […] He gave me a bottle of their Shiraz to bring back, which I might do, unless it gets consumed in Canberra on the way! I also have from Janis [*Laurs*] (who is as generous & lively as ever) an unlabelled bottle of Muscat, & look forward to convincing HM Customs of its innocence.

Can't remember if I told you about my arrival in Mt. Gambier & the missing hold-all full of music, but I had a bad quarter of an hour before the bloke who'd taken it [*by mistake, at the airport*] returned! On the return journey I finally saw a kangaroo – not in the most ideal way, since it was playing with the traffic & was clearly very frightened. It eventually hopped off into the bush, but not before I had the opportunity to conclude that most sheep are, on the whole, brighter….. Not a lot of other flora & fauna, tho' some delightful lizards here in Darwin, & in Adelaide some less agreeable & rather large beasties. No bites, though. The weather has been pretty foul from time to time – Melbourne, on the last day, was icy and wet, and the departure from Port Fairy was in torren-tial rain. Darwin is 100 degrees & very humid, which is a shock. […]

[…] Well I didn't get to see the Jumping [?] Crocodiles – the bus failed to turn up to collect me, so having got to the bus-stop at 6.25 I waited until 8.05 & then wended my way back to bed & sleep. […] It may be my fault, but on the other hand organisation is <u>not</u> a strong point in Australia…..

Anyway, I've had a lovely evening eating a delightful picnic & watching the sunset from the Yacht Club…..The concert last night went well – my page-turner (for the Haydn Variations only) had been to a garden party & apologised for being 'not sober', but he did very well – apparently this one was much milder than last year's garden party, after which […] the Bishop had to be carted home in a wheelbarrow.

The piano was really not all that good, but it is kept in conditions with air-conditioning up to 11 at night, ie cold during the day except when the lights are on, when it gets very hot, & warm during the night because of the outside temperature. Humidity is also a factor. However, the really astonishing thing is that after Cyclone Tracey in '75 (which, as you recall, virtually flattened Darwin) it was discovered full of water […] It's been a very interesting trip, extremely tiring as it developed because of that hectic period in the middle with 8 concerts (inc. 2 concertos).in 8 days, plus lectures & travel. […] I'm certainly keen to come to Darwin again & explore a bit more. […]

John wrote me four two-page letters while on this extensive Australian tour. The above extracts are from the last two. He had been in Brisbane, Melbourne (where he played the piano in the Australian premiere of Messiaen's Sept Haïkaï), Port Fairy Festival, Mount Gambier, Adelaide, Canberra and Darwin. The Melbourne concert was marked by total disorganisation over concert wear. First tails were demanded (though they had not been requested). Then it turned out that neither the conductor nor the other important soloist, Harry Spaarney, from Holland, had tails with them. In the end John wore his white tuxedo and black polo neck sweater, while Harry Spaarney wore tweed jacket and a floral shirt and tie! However, the concert went well and was recorded by the ABC. The winery family were typical of the generous hospitality John received in Australia. The crocodiles John failed to see (whether jumping or not) were in Kakadu National Park. John's hand-writing, always bad, was particularly difficult to decipher in his final letter. The bottle of Muscat did make its way safely through baggage-handling and Customs, back to England, where it was much enjoyed. John was twice bitten by spiders in Australia, once on the finger, by the tiny but virulent white-tailed spider; the other time by the much larger, but less venomous Huntsman.

161

From Jasper Conran
March 24 1994
Typed and faxed)

France

Thank you for the tapes of your music which I have been listening to a lot and which I must tell you sounds wonderful on a very high volume blasting out into the French countryside. It is truly beautiful music which it will be a pleasure to work alongside. […]

Jasper Conran designed the costumes for David Bintley's ballet, Edward II, for which John wrote the music.

162

From Larry Sitsky
March 26 1994
(Typed)

Canberra School of Music,
Childers Street, Acton,
Canberra,
Australia 2601.

I've been meaning to write for a while and thank you for your kind words about The Golem – both in public and in private. Needless to say, imprimata by colleagues are worth a thousand times more than adulation by often ignorant music critics. With those one cannot be selective; if you take the good you must also take the bad! Anyway, I'm now sweating on the CD release of the opera later this year, drawn from 3 live performances, and with a 26-channel recording we should get a good product. […]

John saw this opera by the Australian composer Larry Sitsky at the Sydney Opera House. He was so impressed by the work that he wrote a review of it for Opera Now magazine, January 1994. By a curious coincidence, English composer John Casken had also written an opera on the same subject, at approximately the same time. This also received good reviews.

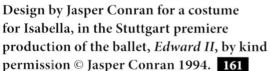

Design by Jasper Conran for a costume for Isabella, in the Stuttgart premiere production of the ballet, *Edward II*, by kind permission © Jasper Conran 1994. **161**

Design by Jasper Conran for costume for Isabella's invasion of England in *Edward II*, by kind permission © Jasper Conran. Designs also used by subsequent Birmingham Royal Ballet productions. **161**

163

From Thomas Pitfield
April 19 1994
(Hand-written)

Bowden

It was good to renew acquaintance with your No. 1 Symphony last evening – I had kept the old Halle programme inside the inscribed copy of the full score you gave me. I thought the 'fireworks' piece came off convincingly too – quite graphic! After a long break I was able to see more of the symphony's virtues; conviction; 'aural imagination', though I must admit that I found the frequent use of harmonic clusters leaning towards percussion – away from the savour of harmony, though that is presumably what you wanted (excuse scratchy writing, I am in the middle of a pen epidemic, affecting several of them (very contagious) […]

Thomas Pitfield was the composition teacher with whom John studied after parting from Humphrey Procter-Gregg. Among Tom's many skills was that of calligraphy. However, this letter is somewhat scratchy and blotchy, though still firmly written. Tom was by now 91 years old. John's First Symphony was premiered in 1965, and championed by Barbirolli. The 'fireworks' piece was a commissioned orchestral opener called Fizzgig, written for the 60th birthday of the BBC Philharmonic orchestra in 1994, and lasting just over a minute.

164

From John to Monica
Nov. 19/94
(Hand-written)

University of Cincinnati,
College-Conservatoire of Music,
Division of Composition,
Cincinnati, Ohio.

Well, it was good to hear your voice this morning […] this evening I'm going out to dinner at the apartment of a student & his wife – very nice of them to invite [*me*] […] Tomorrow is completely free, & I expect to get a lot done: lecture on my 3rd symphony (for which I have to analyse the score!), reading some more of the papers done by my class (which I have to grade), & work on the ballet. The last scene of all, which is quite short & was largely done, or 2/3 done, I've finished in piano score today, cutting & dovetailing & and settling just how long the ending should be….. (Tomorrow I plan to try & complete the full score, which should not be too much of a chore, so I can get on with the bigger stuff in the other scenes of Act 2.) […] The wind symposium people gave me all 8 of the Wind Symphony's CDs! (Customs & Excise will be pleased.) […] one of them includes Nick's [*Maw*] "American Games" in a splendid performance […] Slatkin is doing "Odyssey" in NY (may have already done it by now).

Well, it is now the next day […] Scene 5, Act 2, full score needs about another hour's work now – I have got to the end & merely need to put in the brass & percussion for the ending. It will be a relief to have got this much done, so I can get back to writing the bigger, earlier sections which need doing. My plan for this evening is to write a card to your mother, have a soak in a bath-tub, listen to the 3rd symphony & complete plotting my lecture, & finish Scene 5 . I might read one of the student papers if I have time - some of them are frighteningly competent & filled with numerical tables of various kinds. "Vectoring" is very much the thing with some of them – I understand it but dimly, it having something to do with reducing the intervals of a chord to a number derived from their distance from the root of the chord & then seeing if this "vector" produces a lot of similar formulae in the rest of the piece. My feeling is that it will, simply because a major chord is a major chord is a major chord! […]

John was spending time as Visiting Professor at the College-Conservatory of Music, University of Cincinnati. He wrote me a number of letters during this period. In his first he talks of rehearsals for his Rainforest I, and the Concerto for Piano and Wind Quintet going very well. He likes Cincinnati and his students, but feels that there has been a change for the worse in US society since he first started visiting. There seems to be minimal coverage of international matters in the local newspapers.

165

From John to Monica
Nov. 25/94
(Hand-written)

Cincinnati

[…] this place is like a tomb. Yesterday (Thanksgiving itself) especially. The student refectory is shut for 4 days, & signs of human life are few & far between. This means I'm able to listen to Simpson 9, for my forthcoming lecture, at the proper volume without disturbing the nuclear scientist/brain surgeon upstairs. […] Last night's concert was absolutely stunning. Andrew [*Davis*] (who seemed pleased to see me) was on top form – the Berlioz was magical & powerful, with the most precise rubati & balancing of chords, & the Bartòk Violin Concerto was superbly done by both him & the soloist Sitkovetsky, whose range of tonal colouring was amazing. He played from the music, by the way! […]

John was from time to time criticised for playing from the music. Despite hospitality from the professor, Darrell Handel, students Ted and Elizabeth Trobaugh, and pianist William Black (brother of conductor Robert Black) I think John felt a little lonely in Cincinnati, despite liking it there. It did enable him, however, to do a lot of work on the ballet, Edward II – perhaps an odd place to write a ballet on the violent life and even more violent death of a mediaeval English king, while staying – as he was – in the female dormitory of a university in mid-West America. (He did have to enter and exit through a different door from the female students, however.)

From Angela Simpson
Christmas card 1994

Ireland

Many thanks for your card and news – thanks, too, for John's card from Cincinnati. Yes, the quintet is finished & Bob hopes to now start Quartet No. 16 (via music processor and me!). I'm afraid his pain is no better, which tires him out. If you can ever make it here, we'd love to see you.

Sadly it was never possible for us to visit the Simpsons in Ireland.

1995–1997

From Iris Lemare
Undated, but probably over Christmas 1994
(Hand-written)

No address

[…] I am now 93 – and I am wheelchair mobile, which is a <u>bore</u>. Still swim, but I can only hobble on 2 sticks a few yards. I plod up and down my chlorinated ½ mile once a week which is my only exercise – and not <u>me</u>! I have an electric scooter but it enjoys overturning! Writing worse than usual as it did not like a steep kerb-stone and the right hand is (temporarily) in a bandage. Nicola Lefanu is doing <u>very</u> well at York University – I got transport to Wilfred Mellors' lecture on Purcell there, but couldn't hear much of it – Nicola laid on some wine afterwards. It was great to <u>be</u> among musicians for a brief spell […]

I have a return of the Pitch Defect so I can't <u>listen</u> to Music – the inflections of the speaking voice appear not to be affected but music – instrumental or vocal - is a mess of wrong sounds – I read that Benjamin Luxon had suffered from it – so I wrote to him. He sent me the name of a specialist (Harley St.) that got him back to being a professional Singer. He said that most of the specialists simply say that you have got to "live with it". It just starts – bang – out of the blue. Mine cleared the first time after about a year. This time it has not cleared. Benjamin Luxon said his lasted 2 years. It is for me a great deprivation to be deprived of walking <u>and</u> listening to music. It is not a good idea getting old!

Despite claiming that her writing is worse than usual, it is perfectly clear and easier to read than John's, and the letter is totally lucid.

From David Ellis
4/3/95
(Fax)

Happy 50th Birthday!! No; it's not a case of senile dementia; simply that I've finished the orchestral piece based on your piano work which I've used for a set of improvisations. I know it's nearly 6 years late, but I <u>am</u> a slow writer. […]

See David Ellis's letter of 21/4/86! An exceedingly long six years previously!

From Richard Rodney Bennett
2/04/95
(Typed and faxed)

101 W. 81st

I hope you are deeply impressed, not to say moved by My New Word Processor. I love it, and spend a lot of time typing any old thing on it, since it is infinitely more fun than attempting to write music, which I have entirely forgotten how to do. Funny; I used to be quite good at it. Anyway my friends are thrilled and grateful, as I'm sure you are (aren't you) at receiving long and frivolous letters by every post.

Your letter was a mine of info, jokes etc (or ECT. as you often see). I will deal with the questions re Kandinsky Var. (a rather nasty piece I think now) in a moment, when I have the energy to find a copy. I'm so glad Austr. was a success […] I can't wait to hear the new Symphony […] I'm truly appalled at the idea of doing anything at all to The Mines of Sulphur, though I do see it would be a good thing if I did. Do you ever have dreams in which you are back in the 5th form? Having to take O level? Unable to drink, smoke and all those good grown-up things? I do, OFTEN, and that is what the idea of meddling with the M. of S. feels like. Which reminds me: I stopped smoking FOUR MONTHS AGO; apart from having grown grossly fat and feeling suffused (good word) with virtue, nothing has changed, except that I have stopped having convulsive fits of coughing at embarrassing moments, such as in the middle of a tender and lovely song, or when lecturing to 250 students. Have no inclination to start smoking again; but then again I haven't been able to write since I stopped, so time will tell. Does history relate who the oik was who heckled after Michael's piece. Was it one of those stupid boys who carried on after Harry's opera?

[…] [*a couple of friends*] came to stay for ten (TEN) days, during which I taped fourteen (14) hours of chat. In the course of that week-and-a-half I also did a Weill Hall concert with my oboist friend (Dutilleux, After Syrinx, Telemann etc), two short public service concerts with him, a night in a jazz Boite, a lunch-time concert with a mezzo-sopr. incl. Bolcom, Gershwin, me etc. At the end of the ten days I came out in a FURIOUS RASH from my waist to the top of my head and ULCERS all over my tongue. My Therapist (sic) said it was all stress-related, which is what I thought but didn't like to say.

Talking of stress, did I tell you that I finally gave up the piece which was meant to display every facet of the modern orch. in 20 mins., for young people. As I have found before in similar circs., the world surprisingly does not actually end when one breaks the bad news. I must speak to Ollie about this. But now I'm involved in an almost equally scary project, to be played by SIXTEEN (16) or is it EIGHTEEN (18) orchestras around the UK. And not all at once, either. This culminates in a perf. at Leicester by the CBSO with S. Rattle which takes place on my SIXTIETH BIRTHDAY with FIREWORKS. You may feel that not-so-premature senility has overwhelmed me, and that I am making this up, but I am not. […]

Now I shall deal with the dread Kandinsky. […] There is one VERY odd mistake which you couldn't possibly have guessed: the penultimate bar on P. 9 should be a 2/8 bar with the triplets twice as fast, ie a quaver triplet!!! So, nobody's perfect, except Bouzel [*sic*]. The fourth mvt. was originally written in 5/8, 3/8, 2/8 until I cunningly thought wouldn't it be a good thing to do it all in 2/4, which we found makes it twice as hard, very scary in fact. […]

I MUST stop drivelling on in this unseemly manner.

This lengthy letter runs to three typed pages, about this and that in musical life, in the UK and in the US and even in the Virgin Islands, where the audience was 'a teeny bit confused by the Dutilleux, so thank God we left out After Syrinx'. The 'dread' Kandinsky Variations is a piece for two pianos, which John was due to play in Australia, with Len Vorster, and there were possibilities of recording it. The new Symphony was John's Fourth, Of Time and the River. I cannot now remember anything about John's suggestion regarding The Mines of Sulphur, except that he admired it and thought it should be revived. The heckled piece by Michael Tippett was The Rose Lake, and yes, they were the same 'oiks' who heckled Birtwistle's opera. The scary project with 16 or 18 performances was Richard's Partita, which was highly successful. Ollie was of course Oliver Knussen. And Richard was never grossly fat.

170

To Richard Rodney Bennett
April 2/95
(Typed)

Southall

Many thanks for your fax of today – yes, I'm deeply impressed by your new word processor. Aren't these things wonderful? I've had great fun using my music computer, too – it's fascinating to see the incredible number of different kinds of mistakes one can add to one's repertoire. Many thanks for also answering my questions about Kandinsky (which is NOT "a rather nasty piece" at all but a very good one, so let's have no more nonsense of this ilk, or any other ilk, come to that) and for conveying the information about the wrong rhythm. I'm not sure if this makes it any easier, but we shall see. Anyway, I shall convey the various tidings to Len […] The recording is for a series of CDs which Music Sales in Sydney are starting up, 20th century music of Music Sales copyrights on a mid-price but lavish series with heavy marketing and, they hope (piously), CD-ROM as well. This last will include the composers talking about their music (yes, yes, I feel the same about that), information, pictures, possibly also one's favourite film clips and some crosswords to pass the time. […]

I come not from haunts of coot and hern, but rather from a week of rehearsals for the ballet, and I go back in a couple of days for another week thereof – premiere on Easter Saturday and Sunday. They have TWO orchestras for the ballet, neither of which has yet learnt the piece. We've had rather a saga about the parts, which I will reveal at some later stage – there's going to be trouble about it, I fear. […] I spent one afternoon copying out 197 missing bars of 2nd clarinet! (This is in Act 1, the score of which was delivered to Novellos on

October 19th last.) There are problems with the new technology, including the lack of sufficient experienced copyists, but this surely is a bit ridiculous. […]

Fortunately my extremely limited German is serving very well in rehearsal, and I'm talking fluent gibberish, very quickly. The hotel I was in last week, which I have now abandoned in favour of a proper one, has as its chief selling point the fact that along with your room-key you get a pass enabling you to travel on the buses and underground, ect. [*sic*], while you're at the hotel. It does, however, not have room service, an in-house restaurant except for breakfast […] or, as I discovered when appealing for sympathy on the grounds that I had a cold coming, a kettle or other water-heating device, my request for which caused universal consternation. The bathroom does not have soap – instead there are natty containers for a highly chemical soap substitute on wall-brackets. These are labelled Soap, for the wash-tub, and Shampoo, for the bath, but are otherwise identical. Moreover, one is instructed to Press, at which the whole thing comes off the wall. They mean Squeeze, as I discovered after two days of lateral thought and wall repairs.

It is startling news that you have given up smoking but good that you have no wish to recommence – I wish I could get to that stage. Mines of Sulphur certainly should be done again, by the way, and I absolutely understand your desire not to do anything to it. I think my idea of boosting the string sound is a good one, actually, not just for your piece but as a matter of general practice when there are limitations on the size of orchestra pits - people like full orchestral sound for opera when that was the original concept, rather than having reduced sound.

One final reminder of German efficiency. We boarded the London flight in Stuttgart yesterday evening and were greeted by a stewardess announcing, "Welcome to Lufthansa flight 4056 to Rome". Very nice at this time of the year, I expect. […]

The ballet rehearsals were for David Bintley's Edward II. Composing on computer, rather than manuscript, was a very new thing at the time. John was one of the first classical composers to utilise this technology, and doubtless there were not many experienced computer copyists around. The Stuttgart orchestra's generous work rotas meant that sometimes the players who were at the rehearsals were not the ones who played the performances.

The Mines of Sulphur, an earlier work by Richard, had not been performed for a long time. I believe that John, who admired it very much, had possibly suggested that if Richard reduced the orchestration a revival might be more likely. The sentence about 'haunts of coot and hern' is a quote from a poem by Tennyson.

From Richard Rodney Bennett

08/04/95

Part of a whole flurry of communications from Richard to John or to Monica

New York

Welcome back from glittering Stuttgart. Your letter nearly caused me to be run over crossing W. 81st St., while reading it and (unaccountably) laughing at the same time…..

I will try to deal with the points you Raise. Kandinsky is not exactly a nasty piece, but I do feel with all my music from 15-20 years ago – i.e. After Syrinx, which I've had to play many times recently, while struggling to play the right notes I invariably think, Oh What the Hell Does It Matter, and thrash about to great effect. And I don't think this is RIGHT. P.S. I do, however, think my notes matter a lot more than some distinguished and successful composers I could name, but won't, who seem to have harmonic ears made of concrete.

Which reminds me: I have a very good friend who is a breathtaking young jazz pianist, with a wide musical knowledge, an excellent reader, finger-technique for ever, lovely touch, etc. Well, he and his wife have just bought a Fax machine, and said would I send them their first Fax. So […] I sent a page of [X] at his wildest. So ten mins. later he rang me, seriously distressed, saying But this is NOT PLAYABLE, how can anyone write like that, when it CAN'T be PLAYED – and so on. So I gave him a brief but <u>cogent</u> account of […] the New Complexity boys. He was not at all impressed, but continued to moan disconsolately (the first time I have ever used that word) – But it's NOT PLAYABLE, those rhythms are IMPOSSIBLE […]which may have cast a pall over the christening of the Fax.

[…] I had a new bassoon concerto done a few days ago in London by R. Hickox, the City of London Sinfonia, and the lovely Kim Walker. Everyone seemed pleased. It's the most recent piece I've written (and may well be the last). I'm never sure what to think when I've written what I believe to be the last word in terrifying technical difficulty […] and the player – in this case K. Walker – says Absolutely No Problem, it's lovely to play. I think deep down I want them to be crippled by the staggering difficulty of it all. […]

Thank you for your enthusiasm re The Mines of Sulphur. I have this very good idea: YOU can reduce the string parts for synthesizer!!! Isn't that a cunning wheeze? I have a lot of important things to do, like cooking My Dinner, so will stop.

Richard now had not so much a bee as a hornet in his bonnet about the style of music known as The New Complexity, and its practitioners. He produced some amusing parodies of music in this style, which he faxed through to John, or to me in John's absence. However, though Richard could be wickedly funny, he was never to my knowledge personally malicious. When he finally met one of the New Complexity composers – whom he had not really known before – he found that he liked him very much, and they became good friends. However, he still didn't like the style of composition.

172

To David Bintley
April 29/95
(Typed)

Southall

Just a short note to congratulate you on the enormous success of Edward II in Stuttgart and the superb choreography you made, as well as to thank you for the opportunity of working with you on this ballet. I had a whale of a time writing the piece, and was really moved by the way everything about it fitted together as a unity, thanks to your very strong overall vision of exactly what you wanted to do. I'm having enormous difficulty working out some form of concert piece for the orchestra, but I must do so, and get it off the ground pretty quickly too, if I can. The difficulty is knowing what to leave out, but at least I think I know how it's going to end, which is almost half the battle (I hope).

Will you accept the dedication of the ballet score? It would give me great pleasure to demonstrate in this way how much the whole thing meant to me, and how much I enjoyed working with you. I hope we'll do it again before too long, and will, just in case, start reading up my Morgan.

In the end John decided that the score for Edward II was too symphonic to be made into a concert suite. Instead he reformulated some of it as his Fifth Symphony, subtitled Edward. David was already contemplating another ballet with John, originally I believe intended to be based around Morgan le Fay, but ending up as the two full-length ballets based around King Arthur.

John also wrote his thanks at this time to the Stuttgart Ballet conductor, Davor Krnjak, and to Vernon Handley regarding the premiere of his Fourth Symphony, Of Time and the River, in Melbourne.

Isabella (danced by Leticia Müller) invades England, in the Birmingham Royal Ballet production of *Edward II*. Photo: Bill Cooper. **172**

173

From Richard Rodney Bennett
13/06/95
(Typed and faxed)

New York

Thanks for your letter and I'm so glad to know that your ballet went well, but I have to tell you about the Pandora Guide to Women Composers, which I have bought today in paperback and which has occupied my every waking moment since then [...] As I'm sure you know I am second to nobody [...] in my admiration of certain women composers, but the Pandora Guide does contain quite a lot of hilarious info, and tells one very little about the music. W.C.'s tend to write works with unusual titles: "Summah is the Lovin' Time", "Ocean Motion Mildew Mind", "Up the Ocklawaha", "Maudlin of Paplewick" (which was an opera) , "Percussion Airplane Hetero", "Balance Naked Flung", "Ode to a Morbid Marble", "I'm a Poor L'il Orphan in this Worl'" (1952), "Berceuse de l'Enfant Mourant" ("has all the air of having been written to provide a swift if not sweet ending for the suffering of the child"), "No Chicken in the West End", "Frolic of Elves", etc. etc.

Did you know that –

Frédérique Petrides founded the Orchestrette Classique in 1932?

- that the splendid Rebecca Clarke was thrown out by her father with only £12 to her name, and didn't write at all in the 1930s because she was having an affair with a married man which took all her energies away?

- that Mary Dering's first marriage was probably unconsummated but her 2nd produced 17 children?

- that I was a pupil of Liz Lutyens?

- that Maria Parke (1775-1822) must under no circumstances be confused with Mary Hester Park (dates unknown)?

- that Brahms nicknamed Ethel Smyth "The Oboe" (why?), that Ethel Smyth consoled herself for the loss of Lisl von Herzogeberg with Marco, the first of many dogs, that she had begun to hear ringing and booming in her ears as early as 1913, but died unexpectedly in 1844 (sic)?

- that Emma Steiner spent ten years prospecting in the tin mines of Nome, Alaska, but finally pulled herself together, thank goodness, and wrote a Gavotte for piano and orchestra?

- that Phyllis Tate was expelled from school for singing a bawdy music-hall song that had been taught her by her father, at an end-of-term concert? (Gosh, I do think Miss Briggs is MEAN. I think Phyl was ever so plucky, don't you, Bronwen?) Phyl also had a pseudonym for when she was writing light music – Max Morelle.

- that in 1930 Grace Williams and Betty Maconchy used to sit at cafes in Vienna drinking coffee and smoking the occasional cigar.

- that Priaulx's first work was in 5/8 and ended with a discord.

- More about Ethel Smyth. She blackmailed her family into letting her go to Leipsig [sic] to study composition by refusing to sing or play the piano after dinner, to attend church OR to go riding, till her father finally gave in.

- that Priti Paintal, about whom I now know much more than I ever expected, faced up to Western music with "bewilderment, which over the years has matured into indifference".

Other good titles of works by ladies; "Hall of Machinery, Wembley", "Carrigraphuga" (written for St. Ethelreda's, Fulham), "Quantum Quirks and Quick Quaint Quarks", and "Daisy", an opera about the founder of the girl scouts of the U.S.A.

There is one lady composer about whom I would like to know quite a bit more; she is called Radie Britain, she was born in 1899 and appears to have s.....d anything that moved ("juggling the attentions of both men. On one occasion they both turned up to visit her at the same time.") She did, however, find time to write works entitled "Drouth", "Chicken on the Roof" and an autobiography (get me a copy if you see one) called "Ridin' Herd to Writin' Symphonies".

Priaulx [*Rainier*] (whom I liked very much and who gave me a couple of good comp. lessons, although I couldn't understand a note of her music) played the piano in cinemas and was an air-raid warden.

Now that I've got that off my chest and am feeling more as you might say Comme il Faut, I can begin to answer your letter. I really AM glad the ballet went well and that you had a good time and plenty of fame in Germany [...] I can't wait for the Irish Songbook (B. Rearick will be thrilled) [...] and the 4th Symphony. I'm doing some recitals with Barbara in England in Oct., including a Wigmore. But I think the programme is already set, although there'll be chances in the future. I have a new Rodgers and Hart CD with a splendid singer and Fred Sherry the magical cellist, which I will get to you; the Stan Getz concerto is just out, but apparently copies are unobtainable, which is clever. [...] I'm very excited about the Hindemith; I once nearly had to learn the 1922 Suite, but ingeniously got out of it just in time. There is a rather good German CD of a saxophonist called Hugo Read playing Ernst Schulhoff's "Hot-Sonate" (1930), which is unexpect- edly rather a treat, and NOT brainless syncopating, as one might expect, with a pianist called Peter something who plays the 1922 very well (I think) also some terrible little pieces by Louis Gruenberg called Jazzberries, which is the title of the CD. One of the few piano pieces I ever learned by heart was a fugue in 5/8 from Ludus Tonalis; I also played Amberley Wild Brooks by John Ireland very inaccurately but with a lot of panache (and pedal) when I was twelve. So there.

I can't write music at all any more. I am very shortly going to be publicly shamed.

WHICH REMINDS ME. I finally Came Out. Well, what could a chap do? Gay Times rang Caroline [*Oakes – Richard's agent in the UK*] to say they were doing a special number on 200 distinguished gay and lesbian persons and could they include me. I think Caroline was very very nervous and much relieved when I said but of course. What else could I have said?

So in the May issue THERE I AM, with a full page about M. Tippett, and Max and me sharing a page, with a flattering text AND colour photo, while (this is the good bit) right over to one side is a very skimpy column saying Ones to Watch (about 3 lines each, no photo devoted to [*Richard here names six distin- guished composers whom tact obliges me to omit*]. Ho-ho and Tee-hee [...] MY text (23) lines describes me as a flamboyant figure, which seems odd. Demure, I should have said; or perhaps dignified. Anyway there are lots of famous persons mentioned who don't even rate a photo, LET ALONE IN COLOUR.

I have to stop now and go to bed, so as to be up at dawn all ready for yet another fruitless day trying to write music, which I can no longer do.

Signed Maude Valérie White

Richard followed this letter with another addressed to me, in John's absence, dated 07/07/95, with yet more amusing examples of titles of works. He corrected Radie Britain's 'Chicken on the Roof' to 'Chicken in the Rough' blaming his amateur shorthand.

174

To Richard Rodney Bennett
7th July/95
(Typed and faxed)

From the McCabe Household,
Southall.

Dear Distinguished, not to say Demure, Flamboyance; perhaps I should also add Immensely Gifted and JOVIAL, as it says in the notes for your sumptuous CD with Mary Clere Harlan (for which many thanks – it's a corker). Your various communications are to hand and foot, and have afforded many revelations of inestimable amusement to one and all. The Dictionary of Women Composers that you have stumbled upon sounds to me like a work of fiction – better yet, something edited by Stanley Sadie.

I'm very sorry to hear that you're suffering the slings and arrows of outrageous difficulty with the new piece – I really think this might preface something immensely successful and brilliant. It does happen that way sometimes, though problems composing something can be dreadfully disturbing and depressing. I don't know whether this is the major commission for 115 British orchestras (which I was delighted to see you have got). I shall miss the London performance, unfortunately, since I don't get back from Australia until just afterward, and I would very much like to have been there. I am quite sure it will turn out to be not only perfectly all right, but very fine – it's unthinkable that you should run out of ideas or not be able to realise them properly…..

Meanwhile, Thomas Adès is being acclaimed as possibly "the saviour of British music" – not bad at 24. It was James Macmillan 5 years ago, and George B. before that. I think JM and GB are very fine musicians, but the kind of hype that surrounds things these days is really very bad, and could be destructive for them. However, I suppose it sorts out the people with real determination and character. […]

John was always concerned to encourage Richard, who was getting more and more into deep depressions about his compositional activities. Stanley Sadie had edited the new edition of Grove's Dictionary of Music and Musicians. He was caught out by the inclusion of an outrageous spoof, which passed through unnoticed into the text and caused great hilarity. John has misspelled the name of Mary Cleere Haran, for which he was taken to task in Richard's next letter.

175

From Richard Rodney Bennett
14/07/95
(Typed and faxed)

New York

[…] It is not Mary Clere Harlan, it is Mary Cleere Haran. Mary C. H. has just been to lunch with me, and I had just hugged her goodbye when I collected my mail. Luckily she did not see how you spelt her name.

The last few weeks were so unimaginably despair-making that I finally went to see an ASTROLOGIST, recommended by Mary C.H., who sees her once a year, and said she was sensible and friendly and came up with some interesting things. So she looked at my chart and said if you were going to be Pieceless in August, I would be embarrassed to look at this chart, but you will have TURNED A CORNER BY THEN. I think she means a corner round which lies [*a named composer whom Richard thought little of*], but there it is. Anyway, she said that the next week I would suddenly realise how to write this piece and that then I would be totally obsessed with it. Well, I wouldn't actually put it like that, but I did get up at 2 a.m. and start writing (in D major) and haven't looked back since. Listen, it may be simply frightful, but perhaps public degradation has been temporarily postponed, which is all that matters. It's called Partita, and it is in memory of Sheila MacCrindle, who was possibly the most infuriating person I shall ever know, but also very funny indeed. […]

I don't think I like modren [*sic*] music very much, and am quite happy to leave it all to Paul Patterson, […] Ollie and Thom. Adès. T.A. is a very nice boy, and very bright, but I was unfortunately obliged to do a piece of his with Sarah Leonard (originally for soprano, 2 bass clarinets and D.B. [*Richard continues with various technical and other criticisms.*]

This letter is neither funny nor interesting in any way, and I am very sorry. But it is about 100 degrees and I am sleepy.

Sheila MacCrindle looked after various composers, including Richard, at Chester. When she died, quite young, she was much mourned.

176

From Edward Gregson
19 July 1995
(Typed)

15 Farnaby Rd.,
Shortlands,
Bromley, Kent.

[…] This is really one long thank-you letter, so here goes (in some sort of chronological sequence). Sue and I were really honoured that you chose to dedicate Salamander to us […] I do think it is a very fine piece – for me the best along with Cloudcatcher. It is so full of arresting ideas, so energetic, so integrated and the scoring…. well, anyone would have thought you had been composing for bands all your life. […] I know you are almost an old hand at this now but the scoring really is very individual and so assured…..Then I taped your new symphony from its broadcast – it is so much in my world of compositional thought […] I love the unexpected ending to Part 1 and to the symphony as a whole. […] We share common views of course on many issues – not least tonal structures […] it is interesting that my recent Clarinet Concerto invades this same world of tonal structure, large-scale temporal organisation as your new work. It is also in two parts! Even stranger […] my new piano concerto (which as you know I wanted you to premiere) starts on D and moves to A flat at the end of the 1st mvt! – a bit spooky, no?

177

From John to Monica
Sept./9/95
(Hand-written)

Oakford Apartments,
10 Wylde Street,
Potts Point,
Sydney.

[…] Dinner at Tony Cane's, on Thursday night was very enjoyable. One curious event, out of which I emerged with flying colours. The assembled small company were tested by Tony – a "guess who the composer is" question. He put on this truly awful piano record, & after about a minute I said, "Well, to be honest, it sounds like P.D.Q. Haydn". Tony said, "That's a very interesting reply" – it turned out to be Badura-Skoda playing the fake "re-discovered" Haydn sonata of a couple of years ago! How the experts could have been taken in for a moment I cannot think […] the music is utterly dreadful, quite amateurish. "Skilful fake" my foot! […]

I'm going to stop here – the dryer will have finished, I have time to IRON SHIRTS before Patrick [*Thomas*] comes to collect me.

The 'discovery' of a lost Haydn piano sonata was loudly trumpeted in BBC Music Magazine. John might have been regarded as a suitable person to ask about it, having recorded them all, and written a BBC Music Guide on the sonatas. However, they did not approach him. A small section was printed in the magazine, and John remarked to me at the time, 'Well, if that is the sonata, it would have been better to have remained lost'. By the time he heard this recording, it had already been proved a fake. 'P.D.Q. Haydn' refers back to an LP of Bach on the synthesiser, under the title of P.D.Q. Bach. Tony Cane was, I believe, connected with the ABC.

178

From John to Monica
16 Nov. 1995
(Postcard)

Kansas

Well, as you will know by now, we had my second blizzard of the trip. I bought a kettle & am able to have my teas etc. We <u>must</u> put water-heater on the luggage list! Practising at Barry's house tomorrow […] Very cold and white at moment – power has cut out twice this week apparently.

Barry Tuckwell conducted the local orchestra, with whom John was to play a concerto. I'm not sure whether it was the landscape or John himself who was 'very cold and white'!

179

From Evelyn Rothwell (Lady Barbirolli)
26th March 1996
(Typed)

15a Buckland Crescent,
London NW3.

[…] The Rawsthorne [*Oboe*] Concerto was written for me and I gave its first performance at the Cheltenham Festival. Alan was in a rather drunken period at the time and I have the terrifying memory of receiving the last movement only just in time to learn it, partly en route to Cheltenham! I, too, have great admiration for Alan; any work of his always has his fingerprints on it, and could not be by anyone else. […]

In the same way, though not for the same reason, John received the last two movements of Hoddinott's Fourth Piano Sonata on the morning of the concert, just as he was leaving Cardiff to travel to Manchester for the premiere. He learnt them on the train.

180

From John Pickard
30 August 1996
(Typed)

Forgive the "out of the blue" nature of this letter. We <u>have</u> met in the past – at least once when you gave recitals in Bangor, where I was a composition student of Will Mathias, and also, I think, at one of Bob Simpson's premieres (I was also until recently editor of TONIC, Simpson Soc. Journal […])

[…] The purpose of this letter is twofold. Firstly I intended but failed to write last year and say how deeply impressed I was by your 4th Symphony. I was at the RFH when it was done […] I have been a long-term enthusiast for your music anyway, and think all your symphonies are terrific, but this one really took my breath way […] [I] am bowled over by its power, concentration of thought, clarity of design and sense of inevitability. Having just finished my third symphony (which is also a BBC commission) I would like to think that I am in some small way part of a continuing tradition of symphonic thinking and I have a strong sense of your work being part of that line stretching back through Simpson and Sallinen to Nielsen and Sibelius and beyond. In fact I feel a very immediate link between much of your music and what I'm attempting to do (much more immediate than with Bob Simpson, for whom I have the profoundest admiration, but whose work feels somewhat "remote" in a way that yours does not. I think he turned his back on the world sometime between the 6th and 7th symphonies […]

Some interesting thoughts from John Pickard, who has gone on to have a distinguished composing career himself. His letter continues, asking John's thoughts and advice regarding the use of Sibelius software, which he is considering purchasing. John was among the earliest classical composers in the UK to move on to computer, which, however, he used purely for writing and printing music, and not with an audio function.

John at Abbey Dore in the Golden Valley, Herefordshire, where he finds inspiration for the music for the two David Bintley ballets on the subject of King Arthur, c. 1999. **181**

181

To David Bintley
23rd October 1996
(Typed)

Southall

In between different piano concerts, just a portmanteau note about the two/ three ballets.

EDWARD II: Naturally, I'm delighted it's going in next year's programme, even if the date you gave me for British premiere is when I'm in Australia (and there really is nothing I can do about that, in this instance, though I can at least curtail the planned length of the trip). What I'm writing about now is the orchestration. I'm anxious, naturally, that it should be as practical as possible, and in view of what you said about Romeo and Juliet (which is impossible in one or two theatres), I thought I'd better offer to work out a reduced orchestration for Edward. Perhaps we can talk about this at some time – and perhaps it would be a good idea for me to get together with Barry Wordsworth, possibly in Birmingham, so we can discuss what needs to be done in detail.

My schedule is pretty hectic at the moment, but after mid-November, my playing ceases for a while, and that would be a reasonable time to start working this out. Next year's got some playing early on, and of course new compositions, which will occupy me fully once I get on to them, so the sooner this is worked out the better – it will also mean that you can programme the ballet in as many places as possible. At the moment, it is a huge orchestra – one saving, for instance, might be to have an adjustment to piano/celesta so that they are one player, or even a single instrument with the celesta part written in the piano part and played an octave up. That's the sort of thing I was thinking about.

ARTHUR: I've been thinking, in odd moments, about the scenario, and making a few generalised notes. Until I do some more reading (my library is gradually increasing) and see a more detailed scenario, I don't have a clear sense of who Arthur is – Edward and Isabella were a doddle from that point of view, but things are becoming clearer. I won't be able to do any detailed thinking until I know the person I'm writing about. I think the book you recommended will probably help a lot, actually, and it's being re-printed, so they will eventually let me have it, I trust.

I don't think that it's much use to you to tell you what I've thought so far. I do have one or two overall structural ideas, which we can discuss later, and I suspect, since there are a large number of leading-ish characters, I will need to have a means of differentiating clearly between them. This inevitably leads one to Wagnerian leitmotifs, which I'm anxious to avoid, on the whole, but there are other things one can do (keeping particular instruments for particular characters, special chords, and so on) to the same effect. I have a strong sense, as I think I said on the phone, of the beginning of Ballet 1 being turbulent, active, fast – I even have (which is unusual for me) a specific visual image, which gives rise to the musical idea, but I will keep this to myself, since you will have your own vision. I would merely like to put in a request for a fast beginning!

The only other point I wanted to communicate at this time, as the executives say, is about the Battle of Camlann. Your idea of doing this through the eyes of the women in the story is a marvellous one. My musical reaction is that this needs to be a major symphonic movement, in which some kinds of set structures are used (fairly loosely) – passacaglia combined with fugue, but neither of them conventional in technique and possibly even both of them not clearly audible as such. The inner structure need not be audible to be effective in binding together the various strands. In a piece such as this, the individual characterisation suggested above would be very useful, because it would be clear that the different strands were now being combined and developed finally together.

I also have an idea for the end of Ballet 1: very high, very loud, sustained and open chords (maybe even just a two-note interval) on high trumpets, woodwinds, whatever, with everything underneath it cut off to leave the brilliance shining out not triumphantly but whatever is the opposite.

That's enough for now. This is really to show you I'm thinking about it!'

The Edward II reduced score was quickly and successfully produced, and proved very valuable for touring to theatres with smaller pits. It is remarkable just how clear John's ideas were regarding the Arthur ballets at this stage. David took up the idea of the fast, turbulent opening to Ballet 1; Arthur and Morgan le Fay were represented by horn and saxophone respectively, and the end of Ballet 1 again followed John's suggestion. It is clear how well John and David communicated musically – David was not only musically appreciative, but able to talk in musical language. The recommended book John mentioned was Daughter of Tintagel, by Fay Sampson, an imaginative construction around the childhood of Arthur's half-sister (and enemy) Morgan le Fay, and it proved very useful.

182

To David Sternbach
19th November 1996
(Typed)

Southall

Very many thanks […] for the cutting of the article about Hartmann, which was very interesting as far as it went (was there another page, or was there some poor sub-editing?) As it happens I know the bloke who wrote the book which was referred to at the start […] he interviewed me for the book (in fact I think I'm quoted in it), so it was good to see him getting the credit for an excellent opus. And I'm pleased Hartmann is getting some exposure in the States - would that our composers here were treated as supportively as Hartmann has been in Deutschland.

Very interesting to have your news, and your article on musicians in crisis. Very well written, if I may say, and I believe I understood all the words, which is rare in communications of that kind. It is a very curious phenomenon, this nervous strain and repetitive strain syndrome […] so far as I can see, it is actually avoidable in many cases if people would take time out to think about it and consider what they might be doing wrong, or how they might change their attitude. But it's not so easy I guess. […] I know I like to change the way I compose (hours of work, or technique – different paper and pens, now the computer) every decade or so, and when I adopt a new regime or system I find it very exciting and productive.

For a couple of days, anyway.

[…] Our latest news is very little really – life goes on, with too much to do, but it is all great fun. I've just finished a spell of playing (Ravel G major concerto and several Ludus Tonalises, make that Ludi Tonalii (?) as highlights, plus a particularly successful Trout) so I'm able to get back to the computer and do a few letters before trying to grapple with whatever is next. Hence this unusually speedy reply (only a month – what am I coming to?). One thing I'm involved with which is demanding, and will be stressful before long because it is reaching crucnh point, that's crunch to you and most everybody else, is an advisory group on our big royalty collection business (British version of ASCAP) – they've been told they must investigate sampling all royalties and change their system accordingly, which of course won't work with classical music (well, it doesn't in the USA, and there's less need for it here), and before long the first two phases of gathering experimental data will be complete and conclusions reached. The test is going to be the way we react and the way the big four pop empires react in turn – they actually want classical music to disappear, since it takes bread out of the mouths of starving pop publishers […] So a difficult time may be in store. Fortunately this committee won't last for ever.

Neither will classical music, and I'm the main man representing us against the barbarians, so feel a little exposed. I will have to take my formidable temper under control – no taking empty whisky bottles into the meetings. Though I might need to empty one <u>after</u> the meetings.

[…] I've done my share of directing things, chairing things, presidenting things, so I know how much work it can be – and fund-raising, too. So I wish you well with your American Federation of Musicians – it sounds a tough assignment. My only real worry is hearing loss in my right ear, which was sudden, last year, c. 20% - left ear is spectacularly good […] Scar tissue was blown off an old scar in the ear some time late last year […] I will have to have a hearing aid, just to balance up, though my hearing is adequate – being a musician, though, I notice the discrepancy more than most would. I actually wanted an ear-trumpet, but they don't make them any more.

David Sternbach had changed career from being a hornist to advising on the physical and psychological problems of musicians. John was under very considerable pressure of work, but then he thrived on work. However, note the first signs of his hearing problem, leading to balance problems, and possibly even to the start of the brain tumour.

183

From Gerard Schurmann
December 11ᵗʰ 1996
(Hand-written)

Los Angeles

Thank you so much for sending me the two CDs […] I was bowled over by the music for Brass Band. A complete revelation. I had no idea it was possible to make the medium sound like you do, and write such meaningful music for it. […] Frankly, requests to write something for brass band have always terrified me into total paralysis. Your Edward II score is marvellous. I especially like the way you have managed to preserve something of a mediaeval flavour, which after its introduction at the opening, seems somehow to frame the whole score like a wondrous frieze. […] I am enjoying listening to Ludus Tonalis as I write this, full of admiration and a certain amount of nostalgia because I used to know it very well. […]

I have been busy writing music for a film tied to the usual worrying deadlines and stresses, which is why you haven't heard from me sooner. […]

Carolyn Schurmann, Gerard's widow, has since informed me that the film was The Gambler, starring Michael Gambon. John knew both Gerard and Carolyn, from the earliest days of his career, and he performed and recorded some of Gerard's music.

184

From Sidonie Goossens
23. Feb. 97
(Hand-written)

Woodstock Farm,
Gadbrook,
Betchworth,
Surrey.

I shall be very happy to talk to you about Alan Rawsthorne […] My first husband Hyam Greenbaum ("Bumps" to his friends), Alan [Rawsthorne] and his wife Jessie Hinchcliffe spent the "Blitz years" under the same roof in Bristol until we were bombed from under it! We were then sent to Bedford with the BBC, where "Bumps" sadly died and Jessie and I continued to share a flat, with Alan visiting when on leave from the Royal Army Educational Corps, a period of the war he hated but enjoyed his leave in Bedford, especially during one occasion when I caught mumps and Alan's M.O. gave him six weeks leave. He always blessed me for being a dangerous contact.

Alan was a very gentle and loveable man and when we returned to London after the war we still remained close friends. It was not a happy period for Alan and Jessie [...]

[Sidonie then goes on to talk of the breakdown of the marriage, which she asks to remain confidential.]

[...] our gatherings together would be monopolised by "Bumps", Constant Lambert, Willie Walton and others and Jessie and I would be providing them with their food and wine – Alas! they have all left us [...]

Sidonie also provides a memoir of the Blitz in Bristol, on a separate sheet of paper.

Bristol Blitz

Soon after our arrival in Bristol with the BBCSO Jessie and I got tired of living in billets and decided to rent a large studio in Park St. with ample accommodation for the four of us plus Jessie's spaniel dog and her London house-help – When the raid started early Sunday evening Alan & Jessie were in their room at the end of the Studio with Constant I presume, and Bumps & I were working on some music copying in a small room beneath the studio on street level which we had fitted as an air raid shelter and had stored odd things in for safety including some of Alan's manuscripts, some food and drink and emergency items – We had Jill the dog with us – all nice and cosy – When the sirens warned us of a raid – minutes later we heard the clatter of incendiary bombs like a load of tin cans falling in the street – People started to run down the stairs from the upper floor (which was used as a small social club) telling us to get out quickly as the roof & top floor was in flames – the Blitz on Bristol had truly started – We grabbed all we could carry and I gave Jill the dog a sleeping pill to calm her nerves, and out we went across Park St. to our favourite Pub – the building next door (a furniture store house) was in flames – We found Jessie, Alan & Constant already there, Constant was hosing water on the wall to keep the flames from next door from coming through. We spent most of the time lying flat on the floor while the High Explosives were dropping all around – the nearest ones dropped on the skating rink opposite but mercifully the three consecutive bombs that we heard whistling down were all duds – otherwise that would have been the end of us all….

The next day we had to get out of town – Jessie & Alan went to a cottage in Chew Magna belonging to Julian Herbage and Bumps & I to a farm on the road to Weston-super-Mare where we were billeted very happily until we were moved to Bedford where Jessie and I eventually rented a flat after an unpleasant time in billets. Bumps sadly died in the following year and Alan was away in the army until we all met again [...] in London at the end of the war.

Julian Herbage worked for the BBC, continuing after the war for many years. Alan Rawsthorne later wrote to his father, 'Not even the walls of our house remained [...] Jessie, thank heaven, got her fiddle. Otherwise we have nothing. It is a pity – books, scores, manuscripts – some of them are irreplaceable [...]'

185

To Gerard Schurmann
26th April 1997
(Typed and faxed)

Southall

[...] Many thanks for the various Rawsthorniana, both the remarks about Cortèges etc. and the correspondence with Philip Lane, who I do know slightly. [...] One thing that would be useful would be to have an idea of Alan's artistic tastes outside music – ie poetry, visual art etc. I know something about his taste in poetry, obviously (I'm a tremendous admirer of his setting of mediaeval poetry, which shows extraordinary insight) but there are things that I find difficult. For example, why would he quote Blake as being one of his main interests? The thought has been expressed that this would be Blake's poetry and not his visual work – is it merely the Swedenborgian connection, or is it the massive directness of Blake (which has an almost mediaeval power) or what? Alan's music is, for the most part, distinctly un-Blake-ish, it seems to me. [...] Played Alan's Quintet again not too long ago, with much pleasure [...]

John was researching for his biography of Rawsthorne, and Gerard and Carolyn had been close to him. John opened this letter by sending condolences to Carolyn on the death of her mother. He also regrets not having followed his instincts and gone to New York to visit Bette Snapp, who has just died of cancer, far too young, leaving a husband and young family.

186

From Julian Bream
4th October 1997
(Hand-written)

Broad Oak,
Semley,
Shaftesbury,
Dorset.

I was delighted to have received your letter particularly as it concerned Alan Rawsthorne, a person whom I was most fond of […] With regard to his "Elegy" I will try to recall the events of its composition. I wrote to Alan in the winter of '69-'70 asking him if he would accept a commission for a guitar piece. He wrote to me to say he would be delighted to write a piece for me, but was unsure about the guitar and his ability to write for it. I eventually made a couple of trips to his cottage in Essex to explain to him how the guitar worked in technical terms. At that time I had the feeling that he had another work that he was involved in. However, he did eventually make a start on the "Elegy", and I made a trip to Essex to see how he was progressing. I suspect that this was sometime in early 1971. When he fell ill I did go and see him in hospital, but felt it inappropriate to bring up the subject at that time.

When Alan died I had a meeting with Alan Frank [*OUP 1954 - 76*] to enquire about the "Elegy" & to discuss with him my payment of the commission to Isobel. Alan felt that my commission was only validated if the work was complete. He then showed me the sketches for its continuations and after studying them, I was pretty convinced that the work could be completed. I was also keen that Isobel should receive the commission money in full, as her financial position at that time was pretty precarious. However, I do not remember a meeting with Gerard Schurmann – I certainly met him at Alan's funeral […] to be honest I had no idea that Schurmann also made a version for the work's completion. I would be fascinated to see it. Well, that's about all I remember <u>except</u> that it took me two agonized days to sort out the last bar!!

A gracious letter, and gracious behaviour from Julian Bream. Elegy for Guitar was Rawsthorne's last work. The premiere was given by Bream in 1972, in his own completion.

John unveils blue plaque on the Suffolk cottage lived in by Alan Rawsthorne and his artist wife Isabel, on behalf of the Rawsthorne Society 1998. **185–8**

187

From Sidonie Goossens
3 October 97
(Hand-written)

Betchworth

Thank you for your letter enclosing the extract from your book […] I am very glad of the opportunity to make a few remarks which I feel are important, such as their marriage relationship – You have given the impression that their marriage was unsettled from the beginning and that Alan had had affairs with women throughout their marriage – this is quite untrue – In my letter to you I was referring to the period of their married life <u>after the war</u> […] It was only then that Alan appeared to have other interests and was away for long periods of time and had women friends who interested him more than Jessie – I can't think why this has to be written in a book – <u>Every</u> marriage has its difficult times but why is it necessary to talk about it when both are at peace and cannot explain – We had such happy times making crazy music together – talking and laughing while we waited for the next air raid – <u>and</u> we worked hard. Bumps & Alan & Constant all had to drink and all three had to die as a result - no women were involved – never – but it was the saddest time of our lives – When Alan re-married to Isabel, Jessie would still worry about him and buy his ties and shirts – She was <u>not</u> a down-to-earth housewife – more like a non-appreciated mother […] I have not liked writing like this – but I do mean it – and I hope you will be understanding. I don't know who has given you this information.

188

To Sidonie Goossens
14th October 1997
(Typed)

Southall

Many thanks for your letter […] and the comments on the pages from my Rawsthorne book - I'm most grateful to you for taking the trouble to respond so quickly. I'm also grateful for the story about the Bristol blitz, which is very vivid – I will make some adjustments to that paragraph, though I have to say the difficulty in writing biography (which is why I originally shied away from doing that part of the book) is that one has to choose between different versions of events. Yours is clearly a very strong recollection, and I will, as I say, change some of my phraseology.

From John Pickard
30th June 1998
(Typed)

Easter Compton,
Bristol.

Many thanks for your letter and for the details of what you want saying on your behalf at Bob's [*Simpson*] memorial concert. What you have written seems absolutely ideal to me and I shall make sure it is faithfully incorporated into what I have to say. […] Your letter actually stirred my conscience as I had intended to write last November after seeing *Edward II* at a performance in Bristol. I thought it was a magnificent achievement: obviously the symphonic sweep of the score was the main thing I took away with me. There aren't many full-length ballet scores that you feel you could sit down and listen to just as a musical experience, but I'm sure this is one of them. The other thing that (perhaps paradoxically, given what I have just said) impressed me was that it really felt like total theatre, with all the elements completely integrated. I believe I was hearing a reduced orchestra version in Bristol. It certainly didn't <u>sound</u> like a compromise, but I'll be fascinated to hear the full orchestra version some time.

Incidentally, until my recent house move I lived just a few miles from Berkeley Castle, where the grisly deed took place. The castle is still occupied by the

Poster for *Edward II*, Birmingham Royal Ballet production at the Hong Kong Festival, 2000. 192–3

Berkeley family who, until just a few generations ago, owned an unbroken corridor of land stretching from there to Berkeley Square in London – quite a back garden! You can get a guided tour of the castle from a very nice elderly lady with a well- rehearsed line in decorous euphemism. I am ashamed to say that on the day we visited, a non-euphemistically inclined friend of mine claimed complete ignorance of English history. To her immense credit, she grabbed the bull by the horns and told him!

What a shame you couldn't make it to St. John's the other week. The Salomon made a wonderful job of *Icarus* – they really are a very good orchestra, aren't they? I noticed that *Notturni ed Alba* had been performed by them some months back – hope it went well. *Icarus* was conducted by Philip Ellis, who also conducted the *Edward II* performance I attended – an excellent conductor, I thought. [...]

John had regretfully been unable to get to Bob Simpson's memorial concert, and John Pickard kindly agreed to speak John's eulogy for him. John Pickard had a considerable success with his orchestral work, Icarus. The Salomon Orchestra is one of several extremely good amateur orchestras based in London. Philip Ellis is not only an excellent conductor, but also a first-rate portrait painter, and he was kind enough to present me with a superb portrait of John in pastels, done after his death.

194

From John to Monica
Aug. 20/98
(Hand-written)

Australian National Academy of Music,
South Melbourne,
Victoria 3205.

At last a chance to scribble a few lines. Today has a hole in it, ie no afternoon session, & the young composers are all briskly writing their assignments & the performers rehearsing. So I've come back to the hotel to get a bit of rest & do one or two things (I've just listened to the Barber "Souvenirs" & my Ed. II pieces from the recital Len [Vorster] & I did, on CD, & they sound pretty good – Corigliano and "Basse Danse" still to go).

It has been a very tiring but rewarding week. The young performers are doing a marvellous job. [...] they've had to do 20 works, by 12 different composers, by the end of it! [...] I bought [*on the journey*] what looks like being also useful, a walkman with built-in mike, so I could record on it. Haven't tried recording, but am tempted to try & get an announcement that is repeated every 7 minutes at L.A.

airport: "Attention, Travellers! You are <u>not</u> required to give money to solicitors. This airport does not sponsor their activities." (Also repeated every 7 minutes in Spanish &, I think, Japanese.) After a couple of hours it achieves the status of a mantra, repeated to guard against evil spirits. Also solicitors of course. […]

Another case of England and America being divided by a common language….. *John was writing from Australia, where he was teaching composition and performing at the National Academy of Music in Melbourne.*

A further letter to Monica followed on August 26/98. Among other activities, John had been trying to obtain permission to use a picture by the Australian painter, Arthur Boyd, which I very much wanted for the CD cover of the Hyperion recording of his Symphony No. 4, Of Time and the River. Sadly we did not in the end get permission to use the picture.

195

From John to Monica
Aug. 26/98
(Hand-written)

Australian National Academy of Music,
Melbourne,
Vic. 3205,
Australia.

[…] The National Gallery has nothing to do with the picture, but they sent me to the Visual Arts Department at the Theatre, where a representative took my details and is going to try to get in touch with Arthur Boyd. […] The picture (which I saw) is splendid, & there are some wonderful landscapes in the same area. […] Yesterday I did some useful sketches for Arthur – I'm concentrating on the 1st ballet & Act 1 at the moment. Apart from a couple of sessions at the piano, I've been working at the hotel, & will do some more when I've written this. I don't intend to go out this evening. It is a curious existence, this, rather desultory – I have to pack tonight & tomorrow morning […]

I realise I haven't told you about the recital […] it went very well. I even managed to time it so the town hall clock chiming 8 came in a gap between pieces! The Byrd & Nielsen went splendidly (the Byrd without, I think, a hitch of any kind) & the Saxton was, I think, the best I've done. Brenton's [*Broadstock*] piece went very well (he seemed genuinely pleased), & mine also went excellently. I added the Webern Variations, & even though there were a couple of splashes it went pretty well. Someone said it was the best he'd ever heard. […]

196

From John to Monica
Aug. 29/98
(Hand-written)

Brisbane

Well, a last note before I leave here for Sydney. […] the last I heard from Michael [*Easton*] was Friday morning, when I called <u>him</u> […] Michael was in touch with a couple of friends who had an apartment in Sydney which I could probably have for nothing, & he'd definitely send me a fax by 4pm yesterday. It's nearly 4pm today, & not a dicky –bird. So at 10 this morning I went downstairs, found a travel-agent, & got a hotel room booked. […] I called Andrew & Wendy [*Lorenz*] today. They've had a bit of a time of it. […] Wendy (who is due to play Brahms 2 next week) has strained her hand & is having to rest it) & Andrew, who is conducting next week, is going into hospital for a couple of days […]

Aug. 30: Now safely ensconced in my hotel, which is very comfortable […] There is a real problem with the Sydney water supply (because of the flooding) […] Briefly, we're told to boil drinking water, not to use cold water for rinsing, & to use "normal" hot water (which is actually boiling) for bathing etc. […]

John is getting exasperated with Michael Easton, who as his publisher's represent-ative in Australia is supposed to be looking after him. Michael had always been a very busy and hands-on representative. Probably by this time he was getting overwhelmed by all the work he was handling.

197

From Steve Martland
15th Sept. '98
(Postcard)

Brisbane

Forgive me for being so mean as to send you this postcard because it must look as if I'm gloating. Ha! Actually we've been performing at the Brisbane Festi-val with the band which was a great success. Got a load of Aussie school kids composing and we played their pieces at a special schools concert – a rather rowdy experience. Is it possible to find any human beings as nice as the people in Brisbane? They've been indescribably wonderful hosts. Now I'm off for 10 days at the Great Barrier Reef. It's paradise here. Went 300 ft up paragliding this morning and soon I'll be off jet-skiing. Keep reminding myself this can't last so I'm soaking in the beauty of it all while I've got the chance.

John had just got back from Australia himself, but it is after all a big island. The postcard is of the Great Barrier Reef with a couple of distant white yachts, and a few little white clouds, the blue of the sea and the sky being equally intense.

198

To David Matthews
3rd October 1998
(Typed)

Southall

In great haste (so you will, I hope, receive this before you go away again): keys arrived safely, many thanks. I'm eagerly looking forward to what I'm sure will be a most productive time. Unfortunately the cello sonata premiere is in Presteigne at the end of August, and since they are commissioning the piece, they really do have to have the first performance. A pity, because I'd love to have had it done at your festival!

Re May: at the moment, I'm at the Brighton Festival (presenting a day of Haydn) on May 3rd, and have an (amateur) orchestra performance to attend on 23rd. Between those two I'm currently free, so you have plenty of time to play with for a recital for the festival. I'm delighted you mentioned it, and look forward to discussing repertoire. Have a wonderful time at Macdowall – if you write as much as I'm hoping to during the same period, you'll have lots of fun. And thanks once more for the cottage. […]

David had loaned his seaside cottage to John to work in, while he himself was away on a working trip to the USA. He was also running the Deal Festival at that time.

199

From David Matthews
2 Nov. 1998
(Postcard)

The MacDowall Colony,
Peterborough,
N.H. USA.

Hope you are working as well as I am in this absolutely ideal place. This is my studio, deep in the woods, in which Copland wrote <u>Billy the Kid</u> in 1938, & Roy Harris & Marc Blitzstein were also here in the 1920s (you sign your name before you leave on "tombstones" - pine boards that hang on the walls). I expect to have finished 2 movements of my symphony by the time we leave next week. Lots of brilliant New England sun, but the leaves have almost all gone now.

The MacDowall Colony, from where David sent the postcard, was a place in New England set aside for creative people to work in.

200

From Gerard Schurmann
November 6th 1998
(Hand-written)

Los Angeles

[…] Like you, I too have had a pretty hectic summer going from place to place here in the US. After a short respite we're off to Europe, and will be in England from December 4th – 15th. We'd love to see you both then if only we could manage to co-ordinate a time […] Meanwhile we look forward to the publication of your Rawsthorne book. […] I'm arranging more of Alan's film music (Captive Heart and Burma Victory) for a recording next year. […]

201

To David Matthews
Nov. 9/98
(Hand-written)

Deal,
Kent.

Many thanks for the delightful card – how nice that you've got so much done, & in such lovely surroundings. I look forward to hearing about life at the Colony […] Everything has gone well here. I spent my week back home to good effect, but otherwise I've been here, working away like mad – got an enormous amount of ballet music outlined, & also did a new version of the string sextet piece "Pilgrim", for double string orchestra, which was requested for next February! (Double string was my idea, or were my idea, and should work very well.) So it's been a very successful & thoroughly enjoyable visit.

My plan still is to be here until Nov. 18th, if that is still OK. I'm going home tomorrow (Tuesday) to spend a couple of days printing out so I can check things, & have a performance to attend on Thurs. anyway. I'll return here on Friday. If there's a problem with this, do let me know. […]

202

To David Matthews
Nov. 18/98
(Hand-written)

Deal,
Kent.

Once again many thanks for letting me have the cottage. I wrote a huge amount of music here, & thoroughly enjoyed myself. I hope to be in telephonic communication before you read this, but want to apologise again for the coffee mug breakage – I don't often break things, & in any case didn't really need to use that one (don't know what prompted me to). Tried to find a replacement, but (inevitably) failed. I'm most dreadfully sorry. (There is a poor substitute on the kitchen shelf.) [...]

203

From David Matthews
1 December 1998
(Typed)

Deal,
Kent.

Thank you very much for the chocolates, which I'm eating as I type. I've come down for ten days to work mostly on the computer – I want to put on to it what I wrote at the Macdowall, some of it anyway. I'm glad you were able to get lots of work done, John. Thanks for leaving the house so neat and tidy. Don't worry about the cup; I think I can mend it with araldite – I'm pretty good at this.

Nice to be back [...] though it's rather bleak here, and the wind on the front is fearsome. I really miss the sunlight; the last eight days of our trip were spent in Arizona and Utah, where the sun shone uninterruptedly and the light was so brilliant and clear you could see for a hundred miles. I don't know if you've been there, but if you haven't I strongly recommend it. As well as the Grand Canyon we went to Zion National Park and Bryce Canyon. I don't think Messiaen quite did them justice in his Des canyons aux étoiles – they're beyond description. But he's rather cornered the market in Utah landscape pieces – though I've just remembered that you've written a Canyons, John: is it about this area? We ended up on the way back in an old-fashioned hotel in Flagstaff which was just like something out of a Western [...] Zane Grey had written one of his novels there, and Wyatt Earp had stayed there and shot a bullet into the bar. [...]

John was an avid deserts aficionado. Among his Deserts series, both Canyons and Scenes in America Deserta (The King's Singers) are inspired by the American South West's deserts. Coincidentally, Scenes in America Deserta , set to words by Reyner Banham, ends with the words 'almost beyond description'

From Peter Mountain
5th December 1998
(Typed)

Bingley,
Yorks.

I was indeed the soloist in the Pitfield concerto – with George Hurst and the BBC Northern. I thought it was a fine work, and Angela and I also broadcast his violin sonata. I have a copy of that, but I've searched everywhere and cannot find any trace of the concerto. The BBC asked me to play it and provided the music, and I can only conclude that they must have taken it back after the performance. It was not published, and I had a manuscript part. […] I would love to look at it again. What a terrible shame if it has gone for ever. I didn't know that Pitfield is 95 this year. […]

I enjoyed doing Rawsthorne's "Practical Cats" greatly. I was in the Philharmonic recording of 1954 conducted by the composer with Robert Donat. I thought Prunella Scales was equally good in our performance – perhaps superior in musical ensemble, which is not always easy for actors in these kinds of things. I am looking forward to getting the recent performances of the violin concertos on CD. I remember past performances of No. 1 by Theo Olof and also by Maurice Clare who led the Boyd Neel orchestra when I was in it. […]

To David Matthews
9th January 1999
(Typed)

Southall

Happy New Year! This note has two purposes. The first is to send the enclosed, concerning Edward II and giving details of the London performances. If you and Jean would like to (and can) attend one of them, do let me know as soon as possible and I'll organise a couple of tickets for you. We're going on the first 2 nights – I can't go after that because I have a concerto at Fairfield Hall on 5th (Eddie Gregson's with the RAF Central Band, no less) and a first performance with Chris Austin and Brunel in Bristol on 6th. Quite a week – why does everything happen at once?

The other thing concerns the proposed recital, sort of Jane-Austen connected (thinking about the programme gave me an excuse to read a biography of her, which was great fun and I can see myself shortly embarking on her complete works, when I've finished Proust, if I do). Anyway, may I suggest the following programme (rhetorical question):

Rondo in C, Op. 51, No. 1	BEETHOVEN
Sonata in A	PINTO
2 Nocturnes and Rondo Le Midi	FIELD
Sonata in B flat, K 570	MOZART
Sonata in E flat, Landon 62 (Hob. 52)	HAYDN

This is essentially a programme without an interval, but it's fairly relaxing, so that should be feasible. If, however, you want an interval, I can re-jig the order a bit. In any case, you might want some alterations to the programme, but this fits my repertoire pretty well and seems suitable for the setting.

Field wrote most of his Nocturnes after Jane Austen died, and there's no evidence that I can find that she knew any of this stuff – her tastes (and she did play the piano quite a lot) seemed to be popular songs and lighter pieces. But it should be an appropriate mix of pieces, and I'm assuming you don't want to tie it in too closely with actuality, as it were. Do let me know about this, too, when you can. I will certainly have a lot of fun practising it!

The first performance in Bristol would have been the double string orchestra arrangement of Pilgrim. The Jane Austen-connected programme was accepted by David, as an item in his Deal Festival and the concert took place at Godmersham Park in Kent, a house which Jane had frequently visited. Her brother Edward had been adopted as heir by the related Knight family, who owned the property and were childless.

206

To David Matthews
9th March 1999
(Typed)

Southall

First of all, Happy Birthday! I called this afternoon in blissful ignorance of this occasion, but was delighted to speak to Jean and discover that this was the day. I hope you're having a relaxing day. […] I enclose the programme notes for the Jane Austen concert. They are almost certainly too long, but please edit as you see fit. Also, I've added a general note at the beginning which can easily go, thereby saving some useful space…..

Looking forward to this very much, and to seeing you before then anyway. I hope I might be able to pop in to the rehearsal of <u>Vespers</u> on Saturday if permitted to do so (I know "outsiders" aren't always welcome at rehearsals, and I understand that perfectly well) and if my timetable allows. Good luck with it, anyhow – I'm very keen to hear that piece!

207

To David Matthews
16th March 1999
(Typed)

Southall

Just a short note (rather than a phone call, since they can be disruptive if not essential) to say how sorry we were to have been unable to get to the rehearsal on Saturday. We were actually in Oxford, on the other side of Magdalen Bridge (and already late, thanks to a monumental traffic jam) but not allowed to cross the bridge because of the gas leak alert. We finally got across just after 4, which was too late.

At least we tried! I gather from Martyn Hill that it went very well – he popped into the Holywell Music Rooms after the show, to show Julie what they are like, and we were still there, chatting away. So I shall have to hope that the piece gets done again very soon.

Our show went very well, and was a very nice occasion. As recompense for missing the rehearsal I went to Blackwells [*music shop*], which was, as always, a great mistake, though I managed to buy only two books. A poor show, by my standards. […]

Martyn Hill was the tenor soloist in David's Vespers.

To David Matthews
31st May 1999
(Typed)

Southall

First of all, many thanks to you both for such an enjoyable time last Friday and Saturday [...] I'm glad the recital seems to have been a success. Monica told me about the letter from the Regional Arts man, which simply doesn't make sense to me – your programme this year looks terrific, and Stephen Gutman's recital is a most exciting prospect. I simply don't understand officialdom. Anyway, let's hope the recital [*ie John's*] helped to raise some of the shortfall from the Arts association people.

I must say I was greatly encouraged by having both Dover solo [*sic*] and raspberries on Friday evening – after that I was determined to try and do a decent job! I think I am right in saying that Horowitz always had Dover solo for lunch on concert days, and I understand absolutely why.

Apropos next year: I was really delighted to be asked to do a recital in the Festival next year, and hope this might be possible. To that end, it seemed to me useful if I asked if you've had any of the following works in your programmes in recent years, so I can avoid them (assuming you'd want to).

MOZART	Fantasia & Sonata in C minor, K475/457
	Sonata in B flat, K281
SCHUBERT	Sonatas: in A minor, D784 in D, D850 in A, D959
SCHUMANN	Faschingsschwank aus Wien
	Intermezzi, Op. 4
RAVEL	Miroirs

(The Schubert D959 I played for my University degree recital, believe it or not.) This is not an exhaustive list, but these are pieces that occur as distinct possibles – if there is one that you'd particularly like me to consider from that list, then that'll help. My instinct is to do four works, including a Haydn and one of mine, and the Schubert, if I went for him, would really have to be 784, but if you'd had that recently then obviously I'd work out something else. Miroirs would go rather well on a Bösendorfer – I know at least one pianist who's given up playing the Alborado del Gracioso because the repeated notes are so unreliable on a Steinway [...] but a Bösendorfer would be much easier, I suspect.

Anyway, let me know what you think, and once again thanks for a delightful couple of days. We even completely avoided a torrential thunderstorm which apparently floated across this area during Saturday!

The 'Dover Solo' was a deliberate joke, which had come up during the dinner. David actually cooked the fish, which were fresh and locally caught. Arts associations, programmes and money were always a problem in setting up artistic events. John must have been doing a fundraiser recital for the festival. His preferred piano was a Bösendorfer, unless he could get a good Fazioli. He found the action on Steinways too heavy, and not lyrical in the octave above middle C.

209

From Howard Skempton
8 August 1999
(Typed)

Leamington Spa

Many thanks for your letter and your greatly encouraging response to my accordion CD. I sometimes (perhaps surreptitiously!) listen to these pieces myself, and sometimes even enjoy them, but I find it impossible to pass judgement on them! Please forgive the delay in replying and responding to the marvellous CD of your piano music. I read the excellent review by Michael Oliver in TEMPO and was immediately prompted to write to you, but was overtaken by events.

The CD notes mention "a Bartókian feel" to some of the music of the early Variations and I was struck from the beginning by the "bluesy" play of major and minor which lies at the heart of Bartók's harmony. Elsewhere, so much of the music evokes bell-like sonorities that I thought of Messiaen. I admired particularly your wonderfully light touch (in both writing and playing) at the top of the keyboard (for example towards the end of the Haydn Variations). Michael Oliver is right in his assessment of the Haydn Variations as "among the finest and pianistically among the most brilliant of recent British keyboard compositions" and it merits a permanent place in the repertoire of (other) distinguished pianists (Peter Donohoe, for example). The overriding quality of all your piano music seems to me to be its individual, exploratory character which brings it closer, if not to the "experimentalists", then to a composer like George Crumb.

Howard Skempton's remarks on the CD of John's piano music are both interesting and typically generous. John certainly regarded Bartók as among the great composers but had some reservations about the 'fragmentary' nature of his music. He did remark once that he had 'over-dosed' on Messiaen in his youth. He possessed piano music by George Crumb, but did not, to my knowledge, ever play any.

From Anthony Gilbert
1st September 1999
(Hand-written)

Styal,
Wilmslow,
Cheshire.

[…] Interesting, those Clairs de Lune (titles very Bertrand-esque). Some faint pre-echoes of Gaspard (well, Le gibet, anyway), Debussy, Cyril Scott, even a bit of Holbrooke in La Mer. I see from Grove that he was called the French Schönberg (sic) – presumably they meant that one who has a very dubious association with Victor Hugo. […] I wonder what other music has Bertrand connections. I first read the poems even before I'd been able to hear the Ravel, but they seemed hard to set in my younger years – not that they're easy now, but their structure, and the strange recurrent patterns of assonances and images are a gift. His vocabulary is chosen with immense care – one can see small but significant substitutions from one version to another of the same poem.

John had presumably been discussing the small output of Abel Dècaux with Tony. Aloysius Bertrand's poetry had attracted a number of composers, including Ravel. See John's letter to me of October 28/85.

To David Matthews
2nd October 1999
(Typed)

Southall

[…] we would have enjoyed hearing your 4th Symphony this week. What a pity the Sibelius thing was cancelled! However, we did enormously enjoy your 5th at the Proms. […]

I'm writing about the idea of a recital at the Deal Festival next year. I don't know if this plan is still on, but if so, then I'd like to suggest the following programme:

Sonata in C, Landon 60 (Hob. 50) <u>English</u>	HAYDN
Haydn Variations	McCABE

Interval

Miroirs	RAVEL
Sonata in A minor, D784	SCHUBERT

I think all this repertoire for you is clear, and hasn't been done before. You did ask for a late Haydn, and I've changed an earlier all-Haydn programme so I can include it prior to this concert – it's rather a tricky one.

The programme order has exercised my mind more than somewhat – I hate chronological order, and also feel sorry for poor old Haydn, being put at the start to warm everything up. But my other order was simply to put the second half first, and vice versa – which is fine except that the Ravel really needs to be played once one has got into the swing of the piano, which is why I've put it in this order. If you'd prefer to have them the other way round that would be fine with me, though the Haydn should then be at the end, preceded by my piece.

I'm looking forward to next year, because after I've finished the second Arthur ballet I've got quite a lot of playing, including rather more concertos than usual (not many, but that's still more than usual): Rawsthorne, Mozart and Messiaen so far. Do let me know if the recital is still on […]

The recital did take place, in Deal, on 26th July 2000. We moved house on August 1st, and after getting back from Deal, packed continuously, a marathon undertaking finishing, after an all-night session, at 8am on 1st August, just as the removal men arrived.

212

From Alun Hoddinott
October 13th 1999
(Hand-written)

Swansea

Good to hear from you – I wish we could have met in Presteigne – and I had heard your performance of my piece – for which many thanks again.

I managed to complete the symphony – performed at the end of last month – and the opera – premiere next week. So you know how much mss I filled over the past few months. Anyway, I'm due for a long rest now.

My toe was despatched without any bother or discomfort and I can walk easily again. […]

Alun Hoddinott never dated his letters with a year, but I have allocated this to 1999, when John played his Third Piano Sonata at both the Fishguard and Presteigne Festivals. 1999 was John's 60th birthday and Hoddinott's 70th. Taking on a symphony and an opera at the same time does seem to be a tough assignment.

John cuts a cake, baked by supporters of the Fishguard Festival, to celebrate his 60th birthday and the 70th of Alun Hoddinott, 1999. **212**

213

To David Matthews
8th November 1999
(Typed)

Southall

Many thanks for your letter of October 14th – how I envy you what seems to be your annual visit to MacDowall! I'm glad the recital programme seems OK. The dates of the festival (July 22 – August 5) are fine for me, and I'll keep that period open. If anyone makes me an offer I can't refuse during that period, then I'll consult you about it, but it's unlikely. Sorry to hear about the Brindisi Quartet – a great pity. I've heard them play your No. 6 (which I think is a very fine piece) and was most impressed. Still, I'm sure other quartets will take up the piece.

Life has been very hectic, hence this brief note – recording of Edward II complete last week (Barry Wordsworth and the Royal Ballet Sinfonia, who were all quite superb) left me feeling exhausted. Fortunately some parts did not arrive for me to check, so I had a relatively relaxed weekend (except for the fireworks, which continue as we now have Diwali). The problem of checking the parts remains to be solved, however.....

Living as we did at that time in the very Indian district of London known as Southall, Bonfire Night and Diwali (November 5th for the former, Diwali more of a moveable feast) became a week or ten days of more or less continuous fireworks. The local Indian population being very ecumenically-minded, this combined celebration then tended to morph into Christmas. At the time of writing this letter John clearly had no idea that we would be moving house on the 1st August 2000. See Andrew Keener's note of 16 February 2000 for further news of the Edward II recording.

214

To David Matthews
9ᵗʰ December 1999
(Typed)

Southall

Having learnt (from your answering machine) that you're away until 16th, I thought I'd drop you a line about a couple of things. First, thank you so kindly for sending details of a house in Deal – it looked very promising in a lot of ways, and we thought of taking a look at it, but the lack of a garden (as such) was a bit of a problem. Somehow, once you've got used to having one, you can't contemplate a house without one, and a reasonable degree of privacy in the garden as well. We drove around what seemed to me about half of Kent the other day, just taking a look at various locations, eliminating a few from our enquiries (as the old Bill has it), and ticking off a few as still possible though unlikely (Sandwich, as well as Deal, looked rather splendid). […]

I've just taken charge of a new printer, which it's only taken me 2 days to get up and running. Not bad, by my standards. I had to buy it because one of my printers (my text-attached one, so to speak) finally laid down its life in the service of its country after many years of devoted service. […]

For non-UK readers, 'the Old Bill' is an affectionate, popular name for the police. Sandwich, like Deal, is an ancient town on the south-east coast. A signpost outside the town, much favoured by the light-fingered, points one way to Ham and the other to Sandwich.

221

To David Matthews
24th May 2000
(Typed)

Southall

[…] I enclose revised, ie brutally shortened, programme notes and biography, and hope this is now OK. We're getting into the throes of starting to pack up (our troubles?) ready for moving house – not definite yet, but it looks increasingly likely that we might move during June. At least I should be able to get well settled in before starting serious practice on the Deal programme! I'm also struggling with *Arthur, Part the Deux* - it's rather like walking towards a range of mountains which never gets any nearer. Sometimes, on my bad days (3 bars of useful stuff) I wonder if I took up the right career.

On a more cheerful note, I had an absolute whale of a time doing the Rawsthorne 2nd Concerto last week, and it went pretty well. If the tape is good enough I'll send you a copy – it's such a wonderful piece, and I made no more of a mess of some bits than some well-known people (though probably no less as well). […]

Despite John's pious hope, we were not able to move house until 1st August, as previously mentioned, after a week of frenzied packing.

222

From Yan Pascal Tortelier
Dated only 30th August, but almost certainly 2000
(Hand-written)

No address

I have a terrible feeling that I never acknowledged the recording of "Ludus Tonalis" you sent me some years ago and I'm sincerely sorry about that, particularly considering how we, the Tortelier family, feel about the music of Hindemith: his language, which too many view as austere and academic somehow speaks to us and moves in a very special way.

Stravinsky once said to my father: "Counterpoint is the welfare of music". Well, with Bach, Wagner and Strauss (all Germans…..) he must be one of the greatest ever and your interpretation of the Ludus Tonalis is a real achievement. The Suite 1922 is astonishing too and it is clear that his music speaks to you in the same way as it does to us. Incidentally I once accompanied my father who was performing the magnificent Cello Concerto under Hindemith's baton and

I played for him two of the Interludes (5 and 23) – I was 12 or 13 and you can imagine how I felt when I heard them after all these years. [...]

223

From David Matthews
12 May 2001
(Hand-written)

Clapham Common North Side,
London SW4.

I saw Part Two [*of the Arthur ballets*] last night – I hadn't been able to get to Part One, to my great disappointment, so I feel like someone trying to understand <u>The Ring</u> from just Siegfried & Götterdämerung. But I was enormously impressed with Part Two & especially Act 2 which <u>does</u> have the tragic power of Götterdämerung & provides a real consummation. Your music was consistently splendid, & I particularly liked the Lancelot/Guinevere pas-de-deux in Act 1 – quite beautiful - & the big Act 2 scene, & the end of Act 1 – tremendously powerful - & the music from Arthur's death to the end, which is masterly, every gesture telling (that tremendous Lancelot arpeggio motive!). So, bravo, it's a great piece, & I hope I'll hear it all before too long. David Bintley has done marvellous things too: the whole thing is just so eloquent.

David's reaction to Part Two is very gratifying. My personal feeling is that Part One is even more consistently brilliant, but I especially agree with David that Act 2 of Le Mort d'Arthur does have tragic power.

Morgan le Fay (Leticia Müller) gives Mordred (Robert Parker) a poisoned apple with which to entrap and incriminate Guinevere, Birmingham Royal Ballet production of David Bintley's Arthur ballet cycle, 2001. Photo: Bill Cooper. **223**

224

From Alun Hoddinott
July 29 2001
(Hand-written)

Swansea

I was able to listen to most of your broadcasts last week and really did enjoy the experience. I felt that the enormous range of imagination and technique revealed was so impressive – a rare experience these days! And it was good to have the music concentrated in a relatively short period of time. Many felicitations. It was very pleasant to see you the other day even though for such a short time – a pity it doesn't happen more often.

John was the BBC Radio 3 Composer of the Week twice, in 2001 and 2009. The letter is dated only July 29, but it relates to 2001. Sadly Hoddinott died in 2008.

John with Alun Hoddinott, Presteigne, probably 2004. 224

225

To The Times
February 2002
(Typed. From newspaper cutting)

Kent

In his report on the competition to become European Capital of Culture 2008 (February 11) Simon de Bruxelles sums up Liverpool as having an "unrivalled musical heritage dating back to the Beatles plus visual arts and literature". This does little service to what is actually a remarkable cultural tradition.

Liverpool has the oldest orchestral society in the country, running one of Britain's best orchestras (the Royal Liverpool Philharmonic) in one of Britain's best concert halls, plus not one but two splendid and contrasting cathedrals with fine musical histories and a host of other venues. Educationally it has always had at least a useful musical life, now enhanced by the Liverpool Institute for the Performing Arts, and in the other arts it has, apart from its thriving literary and theatrical traditions, a remarkable and often under-appreciated architectural richness.

But it's the concentration on pop music alone that is so irritating – there's more to life, and more to Liverpool, than that alone.

John rushed to correct a facile and shallow impression of his native city, one to which sadly, however, Liverpool itself seems often to contribute. This is at least the third time that John came to the aid of Liverpool, which however seems currently to have forgotten him.

226

To David and Sally Sternbach
30th July 2002
(Typed)

Kent

Just got an email from you to my publishers asking for my address – shame on you for losing same, but have pleasure in rectifying grievous error. It has been quite a while since we were in touch.

What news? Well, it's a good thing you got me while I've got time to pen/compute a short note! This is going to be a rather frantic next 10 months, and I'll probably not be writing much. It's all playing (or attending performances) – I had to miss a revival of Edward II in Stuttgart a week or so ago because of other commitments, including attending a recording session (my piano music played by someone else, which is much better than me doing it), and I had my first ever Proms commission last week (a 5-minute piece for the King's Singers, part of a group of seven songs by different composers to celebrate the Jubilee). About Pygmalion time too, though I still live in hopes of getting a proper Proms commission before I finally hang up my cricket pads.

During the next few months I have various concert work starting […] in late August at a good little festival over here on the Borders with Wales, playing Judith Weir's Concerto and a crazy recital programme, and going to the USA, Japan and Belgium in the last quarter of the year, a Scottish tour next February, revivals of the two <u>Arthur</u> ballets in March, and possibly, after the last recital of the present programme, some concerts and a recording in Lithuania in the second half of April. A fan-spread of repertoire, which is nice and will be a refreshing change after wall-to-wall composition for the last few years and not a lot of playing.

Composition-wise quite a lot of CDs either released in recent years or in preparation. I do have some commissions for the future, and lots of plans, which include (but this is hush-hush, so I'll put it in code) !@#$%a&* () _ to?X";J9{)!@%*O, which roughly translated means a horn concerto, no less! I shall, of course, refrain from putting any rests in, and am considering the entire thing *gestopft*.

We are settling in, but it's a huge job – my library of LPs and manuscripts is now in the refurbished cellar, upgraded to "basement", which also has an office for Monica – and, as of today, a dehumidifier, which is working away like crazy. A lot of books (most, actually, save for music ones) still in boxes, but being unearthed – wonderful to have an open box filled with old friends now once more available for perusal. […]

David had of course trained as a horn-player. John never received a full-length Proms commission, though towards the end of his life there was the short orchestral opener, Joybox. The Horn Concerto (No. 4 in his Rainforests series) was a BBC commission, but not for the Proms. Tamami Honma recorded John's piano music, and the Lithuanian recording made a superb CD, with Tamami again, and an excellent chamber orchestra under Donatus Katkus. A large quantity of books from John's enormous library still to this day remain in boxes.

227

From Cecilia McDowall
30 July 2002
(Typed)

Thank you so much for your letter, especially as you must be so busy, and thank you, too, for all the kind things you have said about On Angel's Wing. […] Thank you so much, too, for your acute observations on the piano pieces. You have the pedalling idea exactly for <u>Vespers in Venice</u> and I think I may have made the pedalling a little obscure by removing the original instructions. I did wonder whether I was doing the right thing by changing the notation, too, but again, yes please, a sense of freedom would be perfect. And as for bars 68, 70-3 yes, again, the D natural should be a G natural. I think I must had been thinking of D naturalising the sharp of the previous bar and then, unthinkingly, continued with the idea! […]

John was performing a group of Cecilia's piano works at the Presteigne Festival, as previously mentioned.

228

To David Matthews
24th September 2002
(Typed)

Kent

This is really much too early, but I wanted to drop you a line about the Deal Festival and the year 2005. As you know, this is the centenary of a bunch of composers, notably Lambert, Alwyn, Tippett and Rawsthorne. From a purely personal point of view, I'm firmly convinced that the last two are the major figures in this group, and I'm fully expecting (and hoping) that the Tippett Centenary will be properly celebrated everywhere.

However, I'm also anxious that the Rawsthorne Centenary should not be swept aside – he deserves a good showing too. The Rawsthorne Society (which is about to be reconstituted) and Trust are equally anxious, and have set up a sub-committee to try and get a few things going for that year. Though I'm not on the committee, I've been deputed to approach some of my friends in the hope that I can persuade them to pop something in the programmes [...] The problem with Alan is that not everything is equally successful, but at his best he belongs with the best. [...] I'm suggesting the Divertimento (chamber orchestra) and the Concertante Pastorale (a most beautiful piece for flute, horn and strings), and string orchestra pieces (but avoid the *Light Music*!).

Chamber music was one of Alan's greatest strengths, from ensemble pieces like the quartets and the superb Quintet for piano and wind quartet, to duo works of high quality (Violin Sonata). There is also, if you have a guitarist, the *Elegy*, which I think is one of the most beautiful pieces in the repertoire, albeit completed after Alan's death by Julian Bream (very convincingly, too).

This is really just a warning shot across the bows. It might be we can get a chance to talk about this later, if you'd like to – meanwhile, I thought I should put you on notice that I'm on the campaign trail!

John for some reason doesn't mention the completion of the guitar piece by Gerard Schurmann, possibly not wanting to over-complicate things. He adds a PS by hand, asking how David's book on Britten is going.

229

To David Matthews
24th September 2002
(Typed)

Kent

Two letters for the price of one! Many thanks for your message – we were away last week on holiday (for I believe the first time you can probably recall), and had a splendid time in the Lake District. We even managed to get up to Angle Tarn (above Patterdale) which is my favourite place anywhere but which I felt was unlikely since we were very out of condition. However, it is now apparent that to get into condition to accomplish this climb (an easy half-day, according to Wainwright.....), all you have to do is walk down to the newsagent every day!

The other letter is, as it were, a "formal" one about the Deal Festival and Mr Rawsthorne, and is self-explanatory – I felt I should keep it completely separate from this one…. You'll probably want to file it separately, anyway.

This one is really about the Maunsell Forts and the boat trips….. [...]

John goes on to give details about visiting the Maunsell Forts, which are eerie WWII fortifications on the sandbanks in the Thames/Medway estuary. He wrote his last brass band work about them. Wainwright was the acknowledged authority on fell walks in the Lake District.

230

From Judith Weir
5 /10 /02
(Hand-written)

London SE17

I've now been through this – I realised immediately it was going to be totally accurate, and your orchestral reduction made complete sense. (And thanks for improving my Italian – "con sforza" indeed!)

I think I made no marks at all in mvts. 2 and 3, and just a very few remarks on mvt. 1. The one thing I'd like to change (in fact change back, after you asked me about it) is the orchestral G in bb. 324-5. The G in the original f.s. was obviously a lapse in concentration – I was intending to write in octaves – but the G is something I've become accustomed to hearing, and I'd like to keep it in now!

I can't thank you enough for doing this job – I feel the piece has taken a big step forward.

John was due to perform Judith Weir's Piano Concerto in the same Presteigne Festival as the piano recital with works by Cecilia McDowall. The previous piano reduction score had been very hastily made (not, I believe, by Judith herself) and so he took the time to make a new one.

231

From John to Monica
15/XI/02
(Postcard)

Japan

Writing this on the bullet train, looking at Mount Fuji – splendid view! Will see Karen (but not Tak, who is working) at concert tonight. Chopin Pno 5-tet is actually 1st Concerto – works better like this! Cloudy morning, but sun has come out. Rather humid. [...]

This was a Japanese tour John did with the Rubio Quartet from Belgium and pianist, Yoshiko Endo. One of the works was John's own piano quintet, The Woman by the Sea, inspired by a film called Sansho Dayu, by Kenji Mizoguchi. John was talking and lecturing. A dance was also performed to the work in one place. A new composition by John which came out of this tour was the orchestral opener, Joybox, written for the Proms some ten years later. Karen was a former employee at the London College of Music, who had moved to Japan with her Japanese husband.

232

From Barry Douglas
6 – 3 – 03
(Hand-written)

Paris

Thank you very much for the CD and your long letter. You and Monica have written many letters and I always love hearing your news. Excuse me for not writing more. Sheer laziness! The music of Rawsthorne is magical. I hadn't heard much of his music before. Thank you for introducing me to these wonderful works. They are soothing and inventive and very human & personal. Wonderful in this loud, callous era we live in. [...]

Is the 1st piano concerto of Rawsthorne do-able in the string version by a chamber orchestra? I have my own chamber orchestra Camerata Ireland – as you know. In 2005 Cork is the European Capital of Culture. It might be nice to do it there. Also if you have a short string piece or chamber music we could do. […]

I'm not sure if this ever came off. John had hoped, and even planned in his head, a work for Barry Douglas and orchestra, but sadly the opportunity to write it never occurred.

Right: John in Japan, on tour with the Rubio Quartet, for performances of *The Woman by the Sea*, with two members of the Quartet and Peter Mallett, next to John, who commissioned the work, 2002. 231

Right: Poster for *The Woman by the Sea*, Japan 2002. 231

From John Joubert
8/4/03
(Hand-written)

Moseley,
Birmingham.

It was very good to see you up here last weekend. The recital was a memorable occasion – a splendidly planned programme & splendidly executed. I thought you might like to see the enclosed. [...] Anyway, thank you yet again for your performance of my Sonata No. 1: it showed both intellectual grasp & emotional conviction. No composer could ask for more. [...]

John both performed and recorded Joubert's piano music. I think 'the enclosed' was a review in the Birmingham Post.

234

From David Matthews
21/4/03
(Postcard)

Arizona

Did you come here on your Wild Western trip? [*Coffee Pot Rock, Sedona*] It's about as dramatic as the Grand Canyon & we spent the weekend [...] doing strenuous hikes one up a mountainside and the other through a remote and beautiful canyon. What with Californian wineries & Pacific coast & a splendid day in San Francisco we've seen & done an amazing number of things on our trip. John – belated thanks for your response to my piece – which seems ages ago to us – time goes wonderfully slowly on a paid [*indecipherable*] holiday.

To David Matthews, Judith Bingham, James Francis Brown, Robert Saxton, Andrew Nethsingha
4th June 2003
(Typed)

Kent

Gloucester 3 Choirs 2004: Variations

Regarding the above piece, which seems to be progressing so far as the Festival's plans are concerned, I appear to have got myself in the position of moderator (Controller? Gauleiter?) of this particular work – they have assembled what seems to me a very nice bunch of composers, including yourself (this identical letter is going out to you all and to Andrew Nethsingha, by the way…..)

I don't yet have the full details of date, length of variation, fee or orchestration, but I'm sure it will not take long to confirm these – the financial side, of course, is nothing to do with me, but I'll try to get the other details finalised as soon as I can. However, the question of the theme has arisen, and the idea of basing the work on the Tallis theme that VW used for his Fantasia has been mooted. One of our happy band has agreed to it, but another has rooted (and quite understandable) reasons for being unhappy with this, to the extent of wishing to withdraw from the scheme if this is indeed to be the theme. So other possibilities need to be looked at. These seem to me to be (not by any means an exhaustive list) as follows:

1. Another Tallis theme, such as the 40-part Motet. There is a thorough-bass running through this but it seems to me that it wouldn't be a great basis for a set of variations – I did actually write a string piece some years ago based on this work, but much freer in derivation than we are allowed (by law). However, it's a possibility.

2. Howells: a theme from one of his works. The <u>Missa Sabrinensis</u> (the Severn being another obvious connection) is a favourite of mine, and might provide a theme – however, it was first done at Worcester. His <u>Hymnus Paradisi</u> was premiered at Gloucester, and might provide a tune, and it is, after all, an iconic work at the 3 Choirs, as he is an iconic composer.

3. Howells again: there might be an ideal tune somewhere in his splendid "clavichord" pieces.

4. A Hymn-tune: though two of us suggested <u>Hereford</u>, this is clearly inappropriate (I was one of the two). There doesn't seem to be a <u>Gloucester</u> hymn-tune that is well-known. It might, though, be feasible to use a VW hymn-tune such as (probably my preference) <u>Down Ampney</u>.

5. I write the tune myself. This seems to me the worst option, and this isn't false modesty – a tune for this purpose is incredibly difficult to compose, I suspect. It would, however, have the advantage that I could write the tune and go into the first variation, and it would then be simple to allocate fast and slow (and finale) in discussion with you all.

Do let me know what you think, and watch this space for some of the other details.

The village of Down Ampney in Gloucestershire was Vaughan Williams' birthplace, and the hymn-tune for Come Down O Love Divine was very well known. John recorded the Howells sets of "clavichord" pieces, choosing to do so on a light-toned piano. Despite John's humorous missive, he found (composers being very individual characters) the work of moderator (or Controller, or Gauleiter) akin to herding cats. The eventual decision was to use the tune Down Ampney, and the 'very nice bunch' of composers provided a superb and imaginative set of variations.

236

To David Matthews, Judith Bingham, James Francis Brown, Robert Saxton, Andrew Nethsingha
19th June 2003
(Typed)

Kent

THREE CHOIRS VARIATIONS

Since we're not agreed about the theme for this piece, we ought to reach some agreement pretty soon. The feeling seems to be that it should be a pretty well-known tune, and the suggestion has been made of the VW hymn-tune <u>Down Ampney</u>. Howells' hymn-tune <u>Michael</u> has also been suggested, but though a wonderful hymn it seems to me less suitable for variation, and I think it is less familiar, though I might be wrong. I think most of us would be ready to go with <u>Down Ampney</u> anyway, so let me know if you disagree.

It has been suggested I should do linking passages, but I don't think this is a great idea, for several reasons (one of which is that someone is bound to be late!). I propose to arrange the tune and then go straight into the first variation, which I'll do unless anyone objects. We ought to have some idea of what each composer would like to do. My variation, I think, will be sort of moderate and flowing, probably with the tune fairly clearly in evidence, at least in part. I'll leave other people to deconstruct as much as they like! Duration: each variation should be c. 3 minutes (a bit less or more doesn't matter).

John, Monica and Robert Saxton enjoy a pub lunch at the Fountain Inn, Gloucester. Three Choirs Festival 2004. 235–6

Is that it for now? Reactions as soon as possible please, in a plain brown envelope. I am on the internet and learning painfully with many incorrect diversions, but I have an email. […] this will change soon when I go onto a different, broadband system, but it works for now.

John also in this letter set out agreed concert details, such as venue, time, programme etc, possible orchestration, and when the work should be ready. Organising the Variations took up a lot of John's available time. The order, eventually, was Tune, Variation 1 (McCabe); Variation 2 (Saxton); Variation 3 (J.F. Brown); Variation 4 (Matthews); Variation 5 (Bingham). It is interesting to remember how new the internet was, such a short time ago.

237

From John Corigliano
25/06/2003
(Typed)

Forwarded by Schirmers,
USA.

Thank you for your wonderful letter and even more wonderful CDs. What a terrific composer you are! The symphony and flute concerto are dynamite pieces – full of color and passion (I don't get it – you're British??) and craft. The flute concerto sounds so fine – Emily Beynon is first-rate (has Jimmy heard her performance? I bet he's jealous). I am on to your chamber CD (been travelling a lot, so I'm just getting round to enjoying listening to music again). I think Barry Douglas's disc of my concerto is amazing. You know he does it from memory now.....

The symphony was John's Fourth. It is amazing that Barry Douglas played the very brilliant and demanding Corigliano Piano Concerto from memory. Jimmy is of course James Galway, who in fact premiered the Flute Concerto .

238

From Anthony Gilbert
17ᵗʰ October 2004
(Hand-written)

Styal,
Wilmslow,
Cheshire.

In all the mental confusion after that excellent concert I neglected to thank you for saying all those kind things before the superb performance of the Sonata. I was completely taken aback, but generally appreciate your kindness and generosity in saying what you did. As to <u>my</u> generosity, I have to admit that I never <u>feel</u> particularly <u>generous</u> towards my fellow-composers. If I like their work I say so, hopefully in the right quarters, and if I don't, well, I try, not always successfully, to keep stumm. You're a far better example – you go ahead and perform their works.

But particularly, I appreciated your composerly comments on the music. Such observations, perceptions, coming from a composer whose work I also admire, are enormously reassuring. As to the performance of the Sonata, that was finesse and intelligence embodied – it was like rediscovering an old photo, just the way I'd heard the piece when I wrote it, in fact.

The concert was a great success, I thought – one of John's [*Turner*] best, and it was particularly nice to see lots of friends from my younger years, some of whom hadn't seen each other since that time either. Thank you boundlessly for your part in it, and for all your trouble. I enjoyed David Ellis's piece, too – you brought all its poised elegance to life.

This concert, to celebrate Tony Gilbert's 70th birthday, was organised by John Turner, who again has been very generous in his devotion to various composers.

239

From John Lill
January 9th 2005
(Typed)

London, NW3.

Thank you for your extremely kind letter. It really wasn't necessary for you to take the trouble to write but I greatly appreciate your generous words, especially as they come from one so musically distinguished, experienced and full of powerful wisdom!

I cannot thank you enough for your colossal support and deep friendship over so many years. You have contributed so much to my career and I greatly look forward to seeing you soon. Not long ago I heard a marvellous interview with you on Radio 3, in which we heard some wonderful Haydn from you, perfectly played. Your versatility is as astonishing as your natural modesty. […] It was so good of you to write – I suppose it's nice for us to be exalted to the standard of some pop singers and footballers!

This extremely generous letter from John Lill was in reply to John's congratulations on his being awarded the CBE. John Lill certainly needed no support from John in furthering his splendid career.

240

Moseley,
Birmingham.

Many thanks for your letter of 6th January. I was fascinated to hear that you had started a local music society & wish you every success, particularly in these unpropitious times. John Turner has mentioned the possibility of my doing something for him and Craig Ogden, and your request provides a congenial opportunity and venue for us as well as a deadline which concentrates the mind wonderfully! As for a fee don't worry about it – the prospect of writing for such admirable artists will be reward enough (tho' I am a <u>little</u> apprehensive about writing for the guitar!) […]

On July 13th 2005 John Joubert wrote to say that John [Turner] and Craig have the new piece, entitled Duettino. There was also a new work at the ensuing concert by Philip Cowlin, completed by Peter Hope after his death, and the concert was attended by Bridget Fry, who travelled from Merseyside to the south-east of England to hear her little pieces.

241

From David Matthews
15 July 2005
(Postcard)

Can I ask you for two favours. First can you play the <u>Pastoral</u> with Peter Sheppard at our reception concert? I don't think it needs rehearsing, though Peter may be in touch about one. Second, would you take part in the enclosed oddity, based on the "Jenifer" motif from <u>The Midsummer Marriage</u>? I <u>think</u> everyone will just about fit around the piano – we'll have to wait & see. The other performers will be 1) Jenifer 2) William Howard 3) James Fr. Brown, 4) Matthew T [*Taylor*] 5) Colin [*Matthews, and on what appears to be sawboard, David himself*].

David's writing is almost as cramped and tiny as John's own, and is difficult to read. David and Jenifer Wakelyn were getting married. The wedding, and following reception, was a delightful occasion.

To David Matthews
17th July 2005
(Typed)

Kent

Many thanks for your invitation to play the <u>Pastoral</u> at your reception concert – I'd be delighted, and I'm sure Peter Sheppard and I will be in touch about it. Also I'd be delighted to take part in the communal piano work – I'm assuming none of the pianists will be of large build?

Oddly enough, I started writing a piece (for 2 trumpets or similar) to give to you, but it turned out to be rubbish, and I've cancelled it! I'll have another go in the next few days and see what happens. Of course I can't afford to buy you two trumpets, or even trumpet lessons, so perhaps it was a foolish idea.

John did write another piece, Wedding Fanfare, for David and Jenifer, for two solo instruments (unspecified).

John and Peter Sheppard Skaerved perform at the wedding reception of David Matthews and Jenifer Wakelyn, 2005. 242

243

From David and Jenifer Matthews
Dated only 20 Aug. but clearly 2005
(Postcard)

Dartington Hall

We're enjoying our time in Dartington, where I'm teaching 7 composition students of various ages & talents (one is Alissa Firsova who is extremely gifted). They are to write string quartets for a concert next Friday, & we've been also studying string qut. pieces – Webern Op. 5, Stravinsky 3 Pieces, Beethoven Op. 131, so I've been pretty busy, while Jenifer is having a proper holiday, reading & going for walks.

We had a wonderful honeymoon in the Dolomites, with some storms but exhilarating mountain walks, & the last 4 days at Toblach, staying in a friendly family-run hotel above the town with a stunning panorama of mountain peaks from our balcony. We visited the house where Mahler spent his last 3 summers & the Häuschen where he wrote Das Lied & the 9th & 10th Symphonies & it was very moving to be there.

John, thank you for your splendid Fanfare […] I meant to bring the fanfare here, but forgot, so I wonder if you could possibly fax it here […] as I might well be able to find some people to play it. […]

The Fanfare was indeed premiered at Dartington in 2005.

244

From Alun Hoddinott
Dated only March 9, but presumably 2005
(Hand-written)

Swansea

Many thanks for the programme, and for news of <u>Lizard</u>. I don't envy you running a music society – the demands are considerable and seem to be never-ending. It is very noble of you to be doing it – I was glad to put it behind me!

Running the music society did indeed take much of our time – possibly too much from John's point of view, though he did enjoy it. He did not use the society for his own ends. Very little of his own music was programmed. I have not been able to place exactly the performance of Hoddinott's Lizard. I believe it was programmed, at John's suggestion, elsewhere, possibly Presteigne.

2006–2010

245

From Emily Howard
3rd March 2006
(Hand-written)

68 Railway Road,
Urmston,
Manchester.

[…] thank you so much for such a great premiere of Sky and Water – I have enclosed a copy of my MD recording – don't ask why there are 3 breaks because I'm not sure myself!

John included this work of Emily Howard's in his Final Recital, at Presteigne, a recording of which was issued on Toccata Classics.

246

To Tessa Uys
27th June 2006
(Typed)

Kent

[…] I just wanted to thank you so much for playing my Variations at the Ham and High Festival – I remember a very good performance you did on the radio many years ago and was delighted to see the piece is still in your repertoire.

I was sorry not to be able to be there myself, but I was playing a recital elsewhere at exactly the same time – on a 1794 square piano, which was extremely interesting. I was particularly pleased you did the Haydn B minor, which is such a magnificent piece, and I would have loved to have heard it.

Do continue playing the Variations when you get the chance – it's always nice to know that one's music is being played by someone sympathetic to it! I'm only sorry it's taken me so long to write, but my life has been dominated by writing a horn concerto for the last wee while, and this has now reached a stage of near-completion, so I can relax a bit. (Not much though.)

Tessa Uys kindly emailed a copy of this letter to me, when she discovered that I was compiling this book of correspondence. I do remember well the incidence of John's recital on a square piano. It was not something he often undertook, but it was at the request of a friend, whose piano it was, and the recital was given within their house. The programme consisted of Beethoven's Rondo in C, Op. 51/1; Pinto Sonata in A, Op. 3/2; Haydn Sonata in D, L39, and a little suite of teaching pieces by John, entitled Afternoons and Afterwards, which must have sounded quite interesting on a square piano! The Ham and High Festival was the popular short-hand version of the Hampstead and Highgate Festival.

247

From John Joubert
Three letters, between 18/5/06 and 20/8/06
(Hand-written)

Moseley,
Birmingham.

[…] I'm delighted to hear that you'll have a chance to familiarise yourself with the Barber [*Institute*] piano prior to the recording. […]

Thank you so much for the really useful session at the Barber yesterday. […] I have copied out all the new errata you discovered […] During the course of writing them out I discovered a couple of new ones. […]

I feel I must write and thank you for your recording of my three piano sonatas. It was a tremendous effort to fit the whole thing into the space of two days, and I hope you found it worthwhile and not too exhausting. For me it was a unique experience – to hear my work played as I'd always hoped it would be played is unusual enough, but to be performed with such insight by a fellow-composer made it something really special. It was interesting to hear the two first sonatas you'd already recorded all those years ago: I felt the grasp of content and structure had matured & grown even more powerful. And your playing of the big slow movement of No. 3 I found particularly moving. All in all a big landmark for me and one for which I feel greatly in your debt. […]

The second letter contains the bars drawn out in Joubert's hand, with details of the errata. This recording was made for Siva Oke's Somm label, with Siva producing.

at the Presteigne Festival (on the borders of England and mid-Wales, lovely place and festival) as a featured composer, with a lot of performances. I've had a long association with this particular one (and a longer one, though more intermittently, with the 3 Choirs) and intend to give my "farewell" recital there next year, since I've decided to retire from piano-playing (except for Haydn and my own stuff, if anyone wants it).

Why retire? Well, I'm fed up with fighting rotten pianos, which I get most of the time. Practising is getting harder, both in actually playing and also summoning up the enthusiasm. Carrying such a huge repertoire is too difficult, and I can only do that by cutting down to the absolute minimum. I would also like to have a bit of time off! It's virtually impossible to take time off – of course we could do so by not fulfilling our obligations (like the music society which we set up here, which takes up far too much of our time), but that's not how I like to do things. Whether the society will continue or not remains to be seen – we've put our communal feet down and said we need more volunteers or else. The final reason is that I have a lot of pieces I want to write, and if I want to get them all done before I reach 95, when I plan to stop, I will need to get a move on.

Healthwise I have a problem with balance, possibly in both ears or possibly in the right ear (which is the bad one) – it depends on which of the five doctors I've seen I believe. I had one set of exercises I did religiously for 3 months, and had no effect at all […] So now I have a fine collection of walking sticks, which I knew would come in handy one day! They're also very useful for i) carving a way through crowds, rather like parting the Red Sea, and ii) persuading nubile young things to let me have a seat on the tube […]

Our next objective after August is various events (2 performances at the Proms, after years of none), culminating in a birthday concert at the splendid Cadogan Hall in London, with the King's Singers and a brilliant young quartet with whom I worked recently, late September […] And October is very busy piano-wise. […]

An unusually grouchy and tired-sounding letter from John. The remark about the rotten pianos is well justified. We eventually did pull out of the music society, which nevertheless continued for a few years, until put out of business by the Covid pandemic. Sadly John had less than six years left, and died with a number of planned works unwritten, including at least one symphony, two string quartets and a solo piano work.

To David Matthews
3rd September 2009
(Typed)

Kent

This is just a short note to thank you so much for the splendid contribution to the Haydn Fantasies album, unveiled (and superbly played) last Saturday evening at Presteigne. The whole event was truly memorable for me, and I shall treasure it, but I was especially moved by the fact that all the composers had taken care to write proper concert pieces, and of a consistently high standard of imagination and invention.

I loved your scherzando minuet. Very characteristic of you, I think, in many ways (the central section with its trills and the chords, the thirds in bar 60 onwards, the imitative devices and so on) – very tricky to bring off paying tribute to someone like Haydn while not losing your own personality, but you triumphed. I'm also very grateful for the hand-written copy, which again I shall treasure. What a wonderful occasion it all was. [...]

John doubtless also wrote to the other composers of the Haydn Fantasies – a tribute to John and Haydn – namely James Francis Brown, Peter Fribbins, John Hawkins, Alan Mills, Matthew Taylor and Hugh Wood, but this is the only letter of which I have a copy, kindly returned by David Matthews. The pianist was Huw Watkins.

From Colin Matthews
9 June 2010
(email)

In haste, as I'm just about to head for Aldeburgh. Many thanks for your letter. I know Linda [*Merrick*] well, and we've worked with her already on a couple of CDs. This does look like a very good proposal [...] we will definitely look at it at our next artistic panel meeting which will be in a month or two, and I very much hope that we'll be able to give it a go ahead.

A brief email from Colin concerning the recording of clarinet works by John, including the Clarinet Quintet, La Donna.

Composers of the *Haydn Fantasies*, piano solo works written to honour John's 70th birthday. Left to right: Peter Fribbins, George Vass (conductor and Festival Director), John Hawkins, David Matthews, Matthew Taylor, Hugh Wood, Alan Mills, James Francis Brown, with front row, Huw Watkins (piano) and John McCabe Presteigne 2009. **262**

264

To Robert Childs
6th July 2010
(email)

Very many thanks for your nice letter – and for sending the CDs so quickly. [...] The Gaia Symphony is a tour-de-force and a triumph for all concerned – what an extraordinary achievement (including not only the stamina of you and the band but also the composer). And the Elgar Sonata version is outstandingly successful, I think (especially as I've never really been quite convinced by Elgar as an organ composer for some reason – it makes a lot of sense in this costume). The playing is superb, with <u>marvellous</u> warmth and sensitivity [...]

As for the Hoddinott concerto, words (almost) fail me. I really do think it's an outstanding work, one of his finest – good to know (which I knew anyway) that

Alun kept his inspiration burning so brightly. The Concerto for Orchestra, also a relatively late work, is another winner in my view. David's [*Childs*] performance is stunning and makes me very much want to write a concerto for him [...]

As far as a new band work is concerned, I do have one possibility in mind, which is a recomposition of the courtly dances from my ballets on *Edward II* and *Arthur* – the latter is two full-length ballets about King Arthur and there are some dances in these which would work very well on band, and the other, earlier ballet has a set of French Court Dances which would be good on band. The two sets together would probably be about 12 minutes. [...]

The Gaia Symphony was written by John Pickard. The Hoddinott concerto was written for the euphonium player, David Childs, while the transcription of Elgar's First Organ Sonata for brass band was by Robert Childs. Sadly the Courtly Dances idea of John's did not materialise.

265

To Robert Saxton
22nd July 2010
(email)

Just a hemidemisemiquaver to say how much we enjoyed The Wandering Jew – a really fine achievement. What impressed me particularly was the consistent tone of it all – it certainly marks a broadening, or enlarging, of your style, but every bar is recognisably Saxtonian. I haven't heard a lot of your recent music but I think I would have known that it was by you even when the style was more tonally orientated (that is correct rather than "oriented", isn't it?) than usual. The point being that the *mind* is the same.

A large-scale piece of this kind is difficult to maintain, but you did it splendidly. The scenes are exactly the right length, and the flow natural and always gripping. It sounded like a super performance – I hope you were pleased. And splendid singing, too – including that promising young soprano of yours! [...]

Once again, many congratulations. I can see some of the problems you talked about if it were to be staged, but the narrator could possibly move to the front/side of the stage, even sit on a double-bass stool, and "chat" to the audience (which came over very well on the radio), and I for one would love to see it staged.

The 'promising young soprano' was Teresa 'Tessa' Cahill, Robert Saxton's partner.

271

From Bridget Fry
Probably end of 2012
(Card)

Liverpool L19

What a blow. John Turner has just told me your bad news. I am so <u>very</u> sorry. I do hope you get benefit & not too much discomfort from the therapy, and have energy to do what you most want to. I'm so glad we met again at the concert in Kent.

Bridget Fry's card followed news of the discovery of John's brain tumour. Bridget was a harpsichordist, and married to Fritz Spiegl; they were responsible for orchestrating the traditional tune which was used as a theme tune for the TV police series, Z-Cars. Bridget also hastily coached John in playing the harpsichord, when he had to take over playing the solo part in his Metamorphosen for harpsichord and orchestra at 24 hours' notice.

272

From Emily Howard
19th December 2012
(Hand-written)

Urmston,
Manchester

[…] I wanted to write to you before your op., to let you know how much your friendship means to me, and has done since I gate-crashed your piano-lecture/recital at Oxford in (probably) 2000. I really appreciate that you were so kind and encouraging with all my first attempts at composition (and some of my later ones!). And I am more than aware of how much you have done for me, professionally, over the years. I very much enjoy our fabulous chats about composition and composers, and even more so if we are in one of our usual curry-related haunts. So, our thoughts will be with you on 28th December. […]

There were also good wishes from Emily's partner, from John Joubert, Robert Matthew-Walker and others. The operation, which was only exploratory, revealed that the brain tumour was of the most aggressive kind, a glioblastoma multiforme, which is invariably fatal. John rallied from the operation and resumed working, though with intermittent very bad episodes of collapse.

273

From Monica to various concerned friends
30th December 2012
(email)

Thank you so much for your kind concern, which has been very sustaining to John at this difficult time. Please forgive a very multiple update, as it is the only way I can manage to inform so many.

John has come through a very exhausting operation on 28th, and is back home. However, it turns out that they only did a biopsy after all – We probably will not know before Friday 4th Jan. at the earliest what future action will be taken, depending on the biopsy results. Possibly there will be chemo/radio therapy to shrink the tumour, and this may be followed by further surgery. I will try to keep you updated, but please remember that travel times are long, and I spend much time in hospital, as well as trying to keep the household running, and currently looking after John.

Travel over this operation period was catastrophically bad. With Christmas schedules and over-running engineering works, I was spending 6 hours-plus per day in travel, and 6-8 hours in hospital. This should improve in future, but it does mean my time is very limited. The whole treatment of John will, I suspect, run much longer than we first thought. However, the first-class medical team is very positive (and also, it turns out, very musical).

The operation took place at Kings College Hospital, Denmark Hill, London, and it was the medical team there I referred to as very musical. I now took over an increasing amount of John's correspondence, on his behalf. A number of John's most frequent correspondents had now died, including Barney Childs, Alun Hoddinott and Nicholas Maw. Richard Rodney Bennett also died in 2012.

274

To Vlad Bogdanas
20/1/2013
(email)

I was so sorry to have to miss your performance of my Horn Quintet in December – as you know, I was taken ill, and had been looking forward to hearing it (and to hearing your quartet play). I received a CD of the concert the other day – magnificent! Stunning performances of everything (beautiful Mozart and Tchaikovsky, both favourites of mine) and a brilliant one of my piece. I was looking forward to talking about quartets to you and I hope that one of these days I'll hear you do some Haydn, and Dutilleux and Ligeti too – all great quartet writers (so is Tippett!). What a repertoire. [...]

Vlad Bogdanas was the violist of the Quator Danel.

275

To Tamami Honma
26 Feb. 2013
(email)

Last time I was in touch, things were pretty busy and not too bad. They're still pretty busy, I'm glad to say – plenty of CD releases coming out, performances and commissions coming in, etc. I'm currently doing a 7-minute orchestral piece for the Proms – this is after many years of pressure from lots of people to give me a Prom commission. It's been hard work! Fortunately the new controller of the Proms is a friend (his predecessors were antagonistic – one wouldn't even discuss me), and he's done a couple of pieces before.

The irony of the situation, however, is that I was diagnosed in December with a brain tumour. I'm now just over half way through a course of therapy – radio – at a hospital c. 15 miles away across the Downs, on weekdays, and chemo – tablets (many of them!) at home. (The innumerable scans etc showed heart, chest, lungs, stomach, throat and wooden leg to be fine.) So apart from one little local difficulty I seem to be fine. The therapy ends roughly mid-March, and a month later I have what must be a de-briefing from the doctor who's supervising. For the most part I'm surviving OK (helped in the initial stages by some cricket commentaries from India [...])

So we have to wait till mid-April for more definite news about my condition. We were rather overtaken by events otherwise you would have been told sooner. I'm perfectly cheerful about it – since there's nothing I can do about it, regrets would be foolish at this stage, and I have enough to keep me occupied anyway. Monica has done a superb job of coping with the trauma (which for her is probably worse than for me) and the organisation, which is complicated (the regime of tablets is immense, complex and seems to change every week!). She also, of course, drives across the Downs every day. Nice journey, but not our choice in this very cold weather. I start with tablets at 6.30am, with plenty of cold water. [...]

Pianist Tamami Honma had been a good friend and professional associate. She recorded John's piano music, and they even performed duos together. By this time she had moved with her family to live in California.

From Harriet McKenzie
c. end May 2013
(card)

Brockley,
London

Some Greek tea for you, sent with lots of love! We had a wonderful time perform-ing "Spielend" at Bury St. Edmunds. The audience loved it – many people said it was their favourite piece! We have always loved it and are really pleased when audiences get to hear it and love it too! I heard from Philippa [*Mo*] that John has felt very poorly and I'm hoping you are both OK. I'm thinking of you both and sending lots of love.

Harriet McKenzie and Philippa Mo had a violin duo called Retorica. They recorded Spielend, and were also soloists in the CD recording of Les Martinets Noirs. John had a severe collapse on April 23rd 2013, from which, however, he did recover. Harriet was a frequent visitor to Greece, hence the Greek tea.

277

From Giles Swayne
2nd July 2013
(Hand-written)

London NW 10

I have been meaning for some time to write to you, since I know this is a very tough time for you both, and I wanted to tell you how much I like and respect you, both as a composer and as a man. Sorry if this sounds pompous, but it is completely true: of all of my colleagues you are one whom I have always trusted and admired without reservation, and I'm so sorry you are ill. I know that you have a new piece in the Proms, because my friend and colleague John Blood has worked on the score, I think. He tells me the piece is terrific; and I can only marvel that you have been able to work under such difficult conditions.

Please don't think of replying to this: it's simply a way (the only way I have) of expressing my admiration, affection and friendship. [...]

John receives applause for *Joybox*, his last orchestral work, at the Royal Albert Hall. He is seated in his wheelchair in a space above the stalls, with Monica in front, 2013   Photo: Tony Eldridge. **278–84**

278

From Emily Howard
July 2013
(Hand-written)

Bollington,
Macclesfield.

[...] Currently deep into my BBC Phil commission (dead-line mid-August) and so I am completely looking forward to hearing Joybox [...] We enjoy receiving news from Monica about you and are very impressed with your positivity and strength. [...]

The work Emily Howard would have been writing at this time was Axon.

279

From Peter Dickinson
July 2013
(Card)

Joybox a great piece – under the circumstances a miracle. Well done, both of you!

280

From Cecilia McDowall
26/7/13
(Card)

I so enjoyed Joybox last night, full of bright colour, exquisite sounds and a feeling of great fun – loved it!

281

From John Joubert
30/7/13
(Postcard)

Just to say how much we enjoyed your aptly titled Joybox yesterday afternoon (we had to miss the original broadcast). It was a great pleasure to hear such lively and imaginative music emanating from your pen. And what a triumph to have got it completed in time despite the very difficult conditions you must be working under. Many congratulations!

282

From John Casken
30th July 2013
(Card)

I was sorry not to be at your Prom last week but I've been able to listen to it on BBC iplayer. What a wonderfully exhilarating piece it is and so full of musical energy. I loved the way it kept throwing forward new ideas and piling them up. Brilliant! [...] The announcer said that the conductor had raced across to embrace you at the end of the performance, which was a lovely thing for him to have done. [...]

The conductor, Juanjo Mena, did indeed climb off the stage apron platform, push through the arena crowd, climb over the barrier and up the stairs to reach John in his wheelchair, returning I think the same way.

From Joseph Phibbs
1/8/13
(Postcard)

[…] I wanted to say how very much I enjoyed your Proms piece Joybox. Of all the premieres so far, it's been my absolute favourite – the stunning (slightly Ivesian?) harmony at the opening, and the extraordinary way you layer the material subsequently – something I've tried (and failed!) to do a number of times. It had a really compelling and yes coherent shape – but above all it was the spirit and energy of the music which thrilled me. It's going into my teaching repertoire right away. […]

From Colin Matthews
20/08/13
(email)

What a wonderful title for a wonderful piece! I was away at Tanglewood, for the Prom, so have only just caught it on the TV programme – such a joyous machine: I enjoyed it enormously!

John replied in an email dated 18 Nov. 2013, thanking Colin, apologising for taking so long to reply, and adding that '…..titles are the most difficult thing about composing!'

To George Vass
Undated draft, probably early autumn 2013, uncorrected
(For email)

Well, sort of doing emails VERY SLOWLY, anyway! How was the Curlew – a great success I hope (would love to have seen it again)? And how are you – fully recovered from the medical stuff and by now fighting fit I hope.

I'm still not making phone calls (voice tricky), but the last report was a lot better and it looks as if (subject to confirmation) my condition is being managed – the tumour seems to have been diffused largely. I can make plans, therefore!

John, John Joubert and Matthew Taylor at the Presteigne Festival 2013. **285**

About next year Presteigne, I am most grateful for your patience! You usually want some kind of public "do", but I have to say that, assuming I'm around and capable (oh yes), I very much doubt that I could do a panel (hearing, etc). I do have a suggestion for an individual presentation, though, and thought it worth running up the flagpole. It stems from years of people commenting that my music is often moe complex than people think.

I'm thinking I terms of a "Double Man" (as Mellers has VW). You see really do come from two traditions – German music was my first instinct, through my mother, and then I found English music for myself, and the two have always run together, reinforcing each other. Analysis by others has shown a very German approach to structure etc, combined with a very English freedom/impov./fantasia-like approach.

Then there are Coposer [sic]/Performer aspects, urban man with lifelong concern for nature, and other "doubles". I'd very much like to explore his. Personally I think Stephen Jonson would be the person to lead this – I've great respect for his knowledge and insights. […]

I almost certainly sent a corrected email on John's behalf. The typing errors here are John's own. Normally a very capable typist, the tumour was starting to affect his abilities in communication, though not his thought processes, nor his compositional abilities. Probably his drug regime also did not help. The Presteigne session with Stephen Johnson went ahead, and John managed brilliantly, despite being extremely sick the day before, and exhausted afterwards.

From Monica to Michelle Casteletti (RNCM)
11/09/13
(email)

It's very good to make your acquaintance, if only (so far) by email! I don't know if Linda [*Merrick*] has told you anything about John's illness, but he is suffering from an aggressive brain tumour, and it is only fair to outline to you some of his health problems. Firstly, getting him to Manchester will be a major effort (though this will not prevent him, all things being equal!). Walking is very tiring for him, even the small amounts trailing between trains and tubes, for example. The tumour itself is in the area of the brain which controls speech, writing and communication – he has become somewhat dyslexic – hence my taking over his correspondence. February is in any case a difficult month for weather and possibly travel. It is only fair to give you all the bad news! That apart we are delighted and thrilled that the RNCM is planning a celebration for his 75th birthday – it is just a matter of working round the problems, and being aware of them. The best period for us would be your suggested weekend of Feb. 15th and 16th, and if accommodation needs to be planned at Sir Charles Groves House, then may I suggest that we come up two days earlier, so as to give John a clear day to recover.

Regarding workshops, I have to ask you to bear in mind the speech problems. So far John's voice becomes very gravelly, and tends to go a bit, when he becomes very tired, so if he were to give composition workshops, they would really need to be one-to-one, and with an hour in between, so that he can rest. It is a pity that he can't really give class workshops, as he has always loved doing them, but I don't think he could project his voice for that long. As you can imagine, we are very sorry about these problems, from everyone's point of view.

The suggestions you have made regarding music are of course great. I know the artists will play them superbly. Two of them have of course been done not very long ago – but it will be a different intake by now. It would also be terrific for another pianist to play The Woman by the Sea, and if Aaron Shorr is prepared to play this, again we are sure it will be a fine performance. It is also a brilliant idea to get George Odam to come and talk. He and John have known each other for at least half a century, and George is well-used to lecturing.

Hoping that this is helpful to you, and wishing you the very best as you settle in to the RNCM.

Michelle Casteletti was in charge of the arrangements for a McCabe 75th Birthday celebration at the Royal Northern College of Music, of which Linda Merrick was the Principal.

287

From Monica to Madeleine Venner
Oct. 31 2013
(email)

I'm emailing on behalf of my husband, John McCabe, who is of course delighted at the prospect of the commission for Christ's Nativity going ahead. Jenny Wegg at ChesterNovello suggested he call you to discuss the choir's capabilities etc, and I'm sorry there has been a delay in doing this, for various reasons – medical appointments, sorting out major software problems on John's computer, the great storm (!), and yesterday a possible virus on my computer. Life isn't dull!

Yesterday […] John was in fine form, and got a lot of work done, but today, after a not very good night, he seems tired, and unfortunately this makes his speaking voice not so clear. So not such a good day to ring! I am wondering if it is possible to email us […] to give us some indications of the choir's capabilities etc, as starters, and then perhaps John can try calling you when he is in better vocal form. […]

Madeleine Venner was to conduct the Halle Choir in the premiere of Christ's Nativity, a commission for choir and organ, which was to prove John's last finished work.

288

From Kenneth Woods
1/12/2013
(email)

How wonderful to hear from you, and especially to hear you on such good form!

I'm excited to listen to your Hartmann interview. I LOVE his music. I first encountered him on the radio when I heard the first quartet and had to sit in the car until the end of the piece to find out what it was. I've been trying for years to find a chance to do one of the big orchestra pieces, but it's really the sort of thing you need the BBC to support in order to make it happen. […]

I'm very excited to hear your string trio – for some reason I didn't know you'd written one […] it's always exciting to find another piece to add to the list. (The repertoire is not huge, but it's all so damn challenging that you have to rehearse it endlessly.)…..

Tomorrow we record the last of the Gal/Schumann discs, Schumann 1 and Gal 1. Any thoughts or words of wisdom on the Spring? I love it, but also find it the hardest to get inside of the four. Once the dust settles and the discs have been out for a while, my hope is to record Overture, Scherzo and Finale (which I absolutely love), the Konzertstuck and my favourite overtures (Manfred, Geno-veva, Bride of Messina and Faust). [...]

John's String Trio was an early piece (1965), of substantial length (c. 25 minutes)

289

To Kenneth Woods
Undated draft, but end of 2013
(email)

Struggling with writing emails, I'm putting down some thoughts about Composer-in-Association matters in case they come in useful later on. [...] These are not in any special order.

Youtube: brief intros for concerts (assuming I can!). [...]

Pre-concert talks: possibly difficult (depends) – might need help, eg chairper-son or panel. But I can prepare computer presentation (visual) to help to which music might be added.[...]

Repertoire input: [...] Can I recommend works or composers – e.g. a typi-cal spread might include Martland/Berwald/ Balakirev/Sculthorpe/Kulesha/ Rawsthorne. E.g. one thing I did when running the LCM was Delius's *In a Summer Garden* (my favourite of his) plus Anthony Payne's *Spring's Shining Wake*, which is a beautiful paraphrase of the Delius, and it worked well.

Young Composers: Seminars likel to be difficult. Wold be willing, and like to meet young composers and chat informally to them. Also "amateurs" [...]

Performance (piano) simply not possible, sadly.

Ancillary performances/concerts (to present "essential listening") would be great. Finances almost certainly won't stretch to this! Great to do themed programmes, though (e.g. minimalism, jazz, almost anything).

Education: BIG IMPORTANT TOPIC

MISTAKES IN THE UK IN THE PAST WITH RESIDENT COMPOSERS INCLUDED:

Choice of composers too young and inexperienced

Choice of omposers [*sic*] who feathered their own nest and ignored the need for a balanced regime (also happened in the USA!)

Education sometimes too simplistic – kids can often do it!

At least one major composer was wasted: the orchestra in question did hardly any of his substantial works and what he did was mostly arrangements!

If necessary a brain-stormin [*sic*] session! [...]

I have left in John's few typing errors. Despite typing difficulties he was obviously still clear-thinking and drawing on his vast knowledge and experience. Sadly, although John continued working and composing, circumstances during the year, and the advance of his illness, meant that in the end he was scarcely able to undertake any of the planned residency.

290

From Jeremy Jackman
21.XII.13
(Postcard)

The fact is I've all these Byrd pieces as single copies – much more practical for a conductor [...] So I now offer you one of the strangest Christmas presents I've ever sent – a book with the recipient's name already in it!

Jeremy Jackman had kindly lent John a book of Byrd's vocal music, which John had without thinking written his name in. I returned it, with apologies, and Jeremy generously sent it back as a gift. Jeremy, a former member of the King's Singers, who had often sung John's pieces written for that group, was now working as a choral conductor.

291

From George Odam
January 1st 2014
(Typed)

Bath

My first resolution is to write to you! I was delighted to hear both of your voices on the phone recently and I do hope that you have managed to find some happy times together during Christmas and New Year. I was very distressed to hear of the bad time you have both had and so wish I were nearer and could offer practical help, which I would gladly do. I certainly intend to come over and spend a short time with you both later this month if it fits in with how you both are. I will try to make arrangements so that I can maximise my time and take in something coooltural in town. [...]

Being in hospital, even in the best of places, can be a traumatic experience, as I know, although I have been mercifully free of it for most of my life, managing fine as outpatient. After one of my bad early internments I remember that we both went off to Malta together. I wonder if they've finished Malta by now? My recent unexpected four days in the RUH [*Royal United Hospital, Bath*] reminded me and in that short time I was moved twice in the middle of the night [...] But the attention I received and the tests and diagnosis were excellent and the treatments already working by default in that I have been taken off the drug that did wonders for me when I started it 17 years ago when I was reduced to a wheelchair. [...]

This last month has been a good one for me musically since I am not used to attending many performances in a year, if any, so to have four in one month is exceptionally [sic] even if they were all by the same people! Many many years ago I wrote a setting of the Magnificat for Bath Abbey Choir that you were kind enough to look at. You pointed out very tactfully the basic mistakes I had made in writing and I learned so much from that letter. In fact I can honestly say that it made things clear for me that became the basis of my own teaching when, some time later, I became brave enough to undertake it. [...]

George Odam suffered all his adult life from a painful and debilitating spinal condition, despite which his attitude was always positive and sunny. He lived in Bath, so a visit to see us in mid-Kent was a lengthy business. During their holiday together in Malta, George to recuperate, and John in need of a rest, the island appeared to be under major reconstruction.

292

From Peter Sheppard Skaervad
19/2/2014
(email)

I wanted to drop you a line to say how wonderful it was to see you both this week, and to take a small part in your celebrations. [...] Studying and playing your music is a continually life-enhancing activity for me, John. The lyricism, rhapsody, athleticism, fantasy, romance, structure, discipline, freedom – well everything is a complete world which I love to enter. We were all singing your motives and melodies at supper! [...]

Peter was among the musicians who took part in the 75th Birthday Celebrations given for John at the Royal Northern College of Music in February 2014.

293

To Peter Sheppard Skaervad
End of February 2014
(Draft for email)

I was really touched by your email comments – it is inspiring to have such support, and to have it given physical reality by such wonderful performances. It has been enormous fun to work with such superb musicians as you, Linda [*Merrick*] and Aaron [*Shorr*]. Apropos Aaron, by the way, he played Woman better than I have done, and did one or two expressive things which I had done – he does, like you all, know what is going on in my musical mind! (And reveals that there is actually something going on after all.) Have you done the Brahms Quintet with him? If you do, let me know, and I'll try to get to it.

The next para should hopefully not affect any plans we might be thinking about for a new quartet. I fully expect the medical team to keep me going for a while yet (that was indicated yesterday by the oncological doctor who is treating me – it's wall-to-wall medical appointments these days!). News following my recent scan is that I'm back on week-long courses of chemotherapy once a month for a while, the tumour, after a rest, having gained renewed energy – not what I'd hoped, but we hope this regime will enable me to write a few quartets etc! Even symphonies.....? [...]

John had the beginnings of two string quartets and was planning a choral symphony when he died. As previously mentioned, John drafted emails and letters for me to send from now on.

294

To Mark Bebbington
20/03/2014
(email)

I wanted to say how thrilled and delighted I am with your plans for Tenebrae etc. I'm eagerly looking forward to this, and if the medication continues to maintain me in a state of luxury and idleness (well, actually I'm working away!) I'm hoping to make it to Birmingham at the end of April. [...]

Mark Bebbington arranged a piano celebration at the Birmingham Conservatoire for John's 75th birthday, which we did manage to attend.

The BASCA Annual Ivor Novello Award ceremony, where John received a Lifetime Achievement Award, 2014. **295**
Photo: Mark Allan

295

To Chris Butler (Director, Music Sales)
15th April 2014
(email)

Very many thanks for your kind letter about my BASCA award (and what a relief to be able to mention it!). It has taken me an inordinately long time to respond, but only because I tend to write very few letters or emails – writing music is much easier! It doesn't mean I failed to appreciate your kindness.

I was stunned by the award and am looking forward to the ceremony and the lunch very much […] Things are going OK at the moment. I feel very well most of the time, sometimes more tired than at others, but I have no headaches or anything like that – the only problem (other than the main one) is my balance, which has been bad for years but has been exacerbated by the illness. But I'm working away like mad, and have lots of ideas. Composing is genuinely thera-peutic, I believe, and the huge support I've had from my friends and colleagues in the profession has also helped a huge amount. […]

John was given a Lifetime Achievement Award at a lunch and ceremony held by the British Academy of Songwriters, Composers and Authors in London on May 22nd 2014, and made a notable speech, combining insight and humour, which was given a standing ovation. He went on composing almost to the end of his life. The tumour was located in a different part of his brain. Speech, writing and move-ment, however, became increasingly difficult.

296

From Hugh Lloyd
Clerk to The Worshipful Company of Musicians
27th May 2014
(Typed)

1 Speed Highwalk,
Barbican,
London

I'm delighted to be able to inform you that the Company has decided to award you the Iles Medal 2014 for services to the brass band world. I hope that you will be willing to accept this award. […] The presentation of the Medal is usually made on two occasions, first at the British Open Championships and secondly at the Company's Annual Livery Dinner […]

297

To Hugh Lloyd
29th May 2014
(Typed)

Kent

[…]To be awarded the coveted Iles Medal is a great honour, and I am touched by this kind gesture – I shall treasure it. I know my wife has already acknowledged the letter and my enthusiastic acceptance. There is, however, something you should know about my current situation, which is that in late 2014 [*sic*] I was diagnosed with an aggressive and incurable brain tmour [*sic*] […] After various courses of medication (currently steroids – I await the result of the latest scan) the condition appears to be being managed – certainly I am able to work at composition quite successfully.

What it does mean is that travelling is tricky […], though this year I've already been to Manchester (twice), Birmingham, Cambridge, and of course London. The medical advice is that my wife, who is also my carer, goes with me – and takes charge of my wheelchair (I can walk a bit, but not much) […] [I] would certainly like to attend if possible. A lot, clearly, depends on my state of health at the time, but as things are at present I should manage. […]

I have corrected a few very minor typographical errors, other than the obviously incorrect date. John was in fact composing a large-scale work for double choir and organ at this time, Christ's Nativity, his last composition. However, a terrible problem arose while putting the work on computer, with his newly installed Windows 7 (upgraded at their suggestion) proving to be incompatible with his current Sibelius software. The distress of much destruction of work during this struggle caused his health to suffer a serious decline. He was unable to accept the Iles Medal in person at either occasion, and I eventually accepted it on his behalf posthumously.

298

To Howard Friend at Music Sales and John Blood, copyist
26 July 2014
(email)

I am now at the end of my tether, and even if I were fully fit would be so. I am unable to play any MP3s, any Sibelius music files (which include my entire recorded output). I have lost the Character Map, the scanner is not working as well as it was. I am told there are no back-up files (though quite a lot are listed on the Sibelius 6 directory).

I seem to have Sibelius 6 loaded temporarily (another 12 days) but this will not see me to safety. I cannot load Sibelius 5 from the disc I received from them when I reinstalled them some time ago. I'm not sure a restore point would be a good way to go - but in any case I need to delete Sibelius 6, I imagine, since it's not working. At least I have a memory stick with all my Sibelius files on it.

I simply cannot cope any more with this trauma. Is there somewhere [*sic*] out there who could come and sort this out. I have to say that Windows 7 has not improved everything and there certainly seems to have been a serious fight between that and Sibelius.

Sibelius, by that time sold by the Finn brothers who began it, was no help. Every day work would disappear, bar-lines would change, along with sharps, flats, ties and many other indications. We would spend a day working together correcting errors, only to find the next day that they had returned or been superseded by others. After three weeks of distress we were pulled through by the combined assistance of Publishing Manager Howard Friend and copyist John Blood. We managed to transmit a reasonably correct version, in short sections, to Howard, who sent it to John Blood for further correction. John's mental and physical energy broke down through this fiasco, which was the result of being wrongly advised to update to Windows 7. However, Christ's Nativity was saved.

299

Monica to Michael Emery, BBC Singers
28 Aug. 2014
(email)

John would be absolutely delighted to take part in this celebration – thank you for thinking of us. We have been away at the Presteigne Festival and only got back yesterday evening, so much to sort out. It was very hard work (inc. for me), as John has had a difficult summer and has been very poorly, so lugging him about is difficult. However, he did manage a discussion talk with Stephen Johnson, which went very well and was very moving (this was after the previous day, when he had to withdraw from everything, because of a tummy upset).

I don't know who you are thinking might interview John [...] I'm sure whoever you decided on would be good – perhaps yourself??? Whatever, it would be best if it could be done here, as getting John to London by public transport is hard work. We have been up by a local limo service, which was only £65 each way, but even that is expensive. We have some obligations already (some medical) which are settled, or nearly so, in Sept., so dates to avoid would be 5-10 inc., and 25th Sept. Otherwise we have a fairly clear run [...]

This celebration was in connection with the 90th anniversary of the BBC Singers. Michael Emery did interview John himself, travelling to our home to do so. I had made light of John's sickness in Presteigne, when he was very poorly. However, he rallied and did a moving and totally lucid public discussion with Stephen Johnson. Nevertheless this was the last event he was able to attend, and his last public appearance.

300

From Adrian Lucas, on behalf of the British Music Society
2 September 2014
(Typed)

Having recently joined the committee of the BMS and, since August, taken over the role of Chairman to the executive committee, I was shocked and saddened to hear that no-one had had the courtesy to write to thank you formally on your step down from being our president.

Through my time at the Three Choirs Festival, I was always touched by your support and interest in such a breadth of British music, not to mention being moved when you took the trouble to talk with me after conducting Elgar's The Apostles for the first time back in 2001. This was typical of your generous spirit, and an aspect that has also been evident through your association with the BMS. For me, it was also a privilege to conduct your Notturni ed Alba in 2006, with the soprano, Carys Lane. The haunting orchestration and harmonic language was both startling and hugely colourful, and your presence in the audience that night kept us all on the edge of our seats!

I know how appreciative the British Music Society was at your involvement with the piano recordings made for the BMS label. I have just been listening to some of the Ireland and Britten on An English Recital and was struck by the clarity and wonderful control of textures. Lovely too to be introduced to both the Aubade and Gaudì – both strong and dissonant, but also very lyrical and very poignant in places. […]

In summary, may I convey our combined thanks for all that you have brought to the British Music Society over the years, as well as offering our very best wishes to you and Monica – I gather that health issues are uppermost in your minds at present, but we all wish you a speedy recovery.

John had been hurt that, having stepped down through illness as President of the BMS, no-one had written to thank him for his work. John had been a very involved and 'hands-on' President, not merely a titular one. In fairness to the BMS executive, there had been a number of recent personnel changes, and a letter of thanks had presumably fallen between stools. Adrian Lucas's generous letter remedied this. John wrote, in cramped, almost unreadable capitals on the letter, 'REMEMBER SUPREME APOSTLES & NOTTURNI', which I duly passed on to Adrian.

301

Monica to Michael Emery
c. 10/09/14
(email)

Sorry to be slow replying. I am sure you are indeed run off your feet at present. Either day would be good for us – I've pencilled in both 18th and 20th for the moment.

I can't remember if I told you, but John's health took a severe downturn, and he has been diagnosed with a serious DVT, for which he is now on Warfarin, even though it should not be used with steroids. For this reason I've spent many days in the last 2 weeks in hospital visits, usually Medway. John can barely walk, and can't go upstairs (I am trying to find a gap of time to get a stair lift organised) but meanwhile he is sleeping downstairs on a camp bed, while I doss on the sofa – in other words the house is even more chaotic. Despite this he is still bright, and writing music. His voice can go a bit gravelly, but he is happy, indeed anxious, to do this recording, if you are happy. […] We will make ourselves available whenever it suits you, but please bear in mind that it takes me a couple of hours to get us both organised in the morning, as John needs help with washing, dressing, and so forth, so any time before say 10.30a.m. is not really viable. […]

302

From Monica to Kenneth Woods
14 Sep. 2014
(email)

I'm afraid we have been going through a very difficult time, and I'm writing now to let you know that it is possible that we will have a major problem with the October concert unless John's health improves significantly in the next couple of weeks. The trouble for us began when John innocently (and at Window's suggestion) upgraded to Windows 7 from Windows XP, only to find out that this was not compatible with his Sibelius 5 software. Since he had already started a double choir piece for the Halle Choir, and not knowing how bad the effects would be, he had no choice but to plough on with trying to write the piece […]

309

From Madeleine Venner
15/12/2014
(email)

It was a wonderful evening – the Halle Choir gave every last little bit of energy and passion in their performance, and they felt so wonderful about singing such an incredible piece. The audience feedback was terrific, and so many people said that it was the best new work they can remember having heard – so exciting, so thrilling.[…]

310

From John Blood
16/12/2014
(email)

I have only just seen your email, which affected me deeply. […] I don't know what to say about the terrible time you and John are experiencing, except that my heart goes out to you both. […] That John is still scribbling music says so much of the spirit that permeates so much of his music. Of all the composers that I've worked for he is the one that seems to be so in touch with the real world and real, human emotions. […]

311

From Monica to Jonathan Scott
6/01/15
(email)

It has been on my mind and conscience that we have not yet thanked you for the tremendous part you played in the premiere of Christ's Nativity. It was not forgotten about, but although I was able to thank Madeleine, as I already had an email address for her, I hadn't one for you and at first wasn't able to obtain one […] Without going on with excuses, life is pretty difficult for me at present, as I have 24/7 responsibility for John, who is helpless without me […]

Jonathan Scott, who was the organist for the premiere, replied very kindly. John and I had by now received a CD of the premiere performance.

From Richard Evans
15th January 2015
(Typed)

Longton,
Preston.

[…] In November of last year, as a liveryman of the Worshipful Company [of Musicians], I attended the Installation Dinner at Drapers Hall fully expecting to see my dear friend, John, receive the Iles Medal for his services to brass bands. My anticipation soon turned to sorrow when I was told that John would not be there, due to his rather serious illness. […]

Thank you, John, for bringing happiness, excitement, sheer beauty of sound and form in your music for all of us working musicians and followers.

Richard Evans was one of the leading brass band musical directors. He conducted the Leyland Band in Cloudcatcher Fells when it was the test-piece for the National Brass Band Championship at the Royal Albert Hall.

313

To Michael Emery and BBC Singers
Undated draft

To reach the pinnacle of your profession at the start of your career is a remarkable achievement. To stay at the top and see off the competition is astonishing. Longevity in choirs is more astonishing still. There are ways in which this can be achieved, of course, but it requires constant eagle-eyed (and I suppose eagle-eared) supervision and quality control, or the sensitive changing of personnel – singers and guest musicians, conductors and managements.

In all these respects the BBC Singers have been pre-eminently successful in recent decades. And from the first conductor (Leslie Woodgate) onwards to David Hill they have had outstanding directors for whom the word "genius" would not be extravagant. Their musical and technical expertise enables them to perform the most difficult new music as if it were standard repertoire.

As a result of these skills, their vast and all-encompassing repertoire enables them to give possibly the most exciting performances and programmes on the planet, introducing audiences to music of rare quality, and often supreme virtuosity – and always of communicative power.

Happy Birthday.

This letter from John was requested by Michael Emery as part of the celebration of the 90th Anniversary of the BBC Singers. John wrote the letter in draft, and I typed it for him. The sentence prior to the last paragraph is written as an addition, on the back of the draft, in my hand-writing, but was dictated by John.

314

John's last letter
Draft c. Christmas 2014

Dear Friends,

It has been such a long time since I was in touch, but, as will become obvious, there are good reasons for this. I do apologise for my silence, though, because I have continued to receive copious good wishes, presents, and strong, encouraging support.

Following my Prom in 2021 [*sic*] – JOYBOX – I had some good times, but a physical collapse in autumn 2013 left me very weak, and it took me a while to recover. However, I was able to pick up in time for some truly wonderful celebrations for my 75th birthday year, for which I thank you all, once again. Among these very special events was my complete piano music in a festival at the RNCM. I wish I could mention all the wonderful performances and tributes, which have meant so much to me.

I managed to get back to composition, in the early part of this year, writing a work for trumpet and piano (Simon Desbruslais and Clare Hammond) and a choral work for double choir/organ (Halle Choir) […]

John here digresses to describe his software problems, and also his unhappy stay in Medway hospital.

I am now back home under hospice conditions and hopefully gradually recovering from the decline which set in, in hospital […] I am trying to get back to composing, working on a couple of pieces, though we still have to solve the software problems, sadly.

Throughout the whole of this experience I have been deeply moved by the support I have received, and by such warm and committed friendship. Needless to say, I am delighted to hear from you whenever you have time, though writing and talking are still hard for me.

John's last letter was composed as an update to be sent to friends. Written in cramped, small capital letters, it contains misspellings and many repetitions of individual letters. The latter part of the letter was dictated to me. He did not manage to complete any further composition, despite visits from George Odam and former LCM student Anthony Davie to try to assist him. John told me that his final composition, a setting of the words from *King Lear*, spoken on the 'blasted heath' was completed, and perhaps it was, in his head, but he was unable to write it down.

In early 2015 John was taken back to hospital. After a while he was removed to a nearby hospice, where he died around midnight on 13th – 14th February. I wrote to inform many of his friends, often in separate emails. The following was the first, sent to George Odam, and to Andrew Keener and Peter Avis, and it serves as an example.

(email)

This is to let you know that John died at the hospice at 1 a.m. this morning. I am too shocked at present to say much more. I have a lot of things to do this morning, so will be out of the house. I hope I can live up to what he was, and what he meant to me. Peter, I have to think ahead to funeral arrangements. I know I want a lot of music – music, after all, was what John was. Might Andrew have time to make a suitable CD to be played, if I can get hold of the relevant ones here. If he is too tied up I can probably make other arrangements. John himself did these things for my mother and brother, but I don't have the capability I'm afraid.

There are errors in my typing, from exhaustion and shock. John had been alert and in good spirits when he was taken to the hospice a few days earlier, deeply relieved to be out of the hospital, where he had been very unhappy.

Andrew Keener kindly put together a music CD for me.

Byrd: Ave verum corpus

Tippett: from A Child of our Time – How can I cherish my man?; Steal away

McCabe: Proud Songsters

Hindemith: Ludus Tonalis – Fuga Duodecima in F sharp

Nielsen: Five Piano Pieces, Op. 3, No. 1

Haydn: Piano Sonata, Landon 38 – Adagio

Vaughan Williams: Five Tudor Portraits – Lament for Philip Sparrow – final section, beginning 'And now the dark cloudy night…'

The Tippett had been his own choice. The Hindemith fugue he felt was the most beautiful ever written. The Nielsen was not a totally satisfactory choice, but I felt Nielsen should be represented, and could not include the whole of one of the great works, such as the Chaconne. The brief setting of Hardy's Proud Songsters illustrates the transitory nature of life. The Haydn Sonata movement was of course from his complete recording set. Vaughan Williams' Five Tudor Portraits was a favourite of both of us. The Lament for Philip Sparrow turns from a child's fantasy to a lament for all sorrowing mankind. I was told (I could not see it for myself), that at the words, 'And now the dark cloudy night', a shadow passed over the sun, leaving an eerie darkness.

PAGE INDEX OF CORRESPONDENTS

Also available from Forsyth, a magnificent, fully illustrated volume detailing the life and work of Thomas Pitfield, composer, artist, craftsman, poet.

Endless Fascination

"Thomas Pitfield (1903–99) can best be described as a 20th century Renaissance man"

British Music Society News

Forsyth Est 1857

ISBN: 978-0-9514795-4-4